City Essentials

A Glossary of
Financial Terms

LEARNING MEDIA

Published September 2008

ISBN 978 07517 5391 2

British Library Cataloguing-in-Publication Data
A catalogue record for this book
is available from the British Library

Published by

BPP Learning Media Ltd
BPP House, Aldine Place
London W12 8AA

www.bpp.com/learningmedia

Cover photo by Terence O'Loughlin

Printed in Great Britain by Martins the Printers

Your learning materials, published by BPP Learning Media,
are printed on paper sourced from sustainable, managed
forests.

£40.00

48-hour rule. The requirement that a company seeking a listing should submit any documents required in their final form, to the UK *Listings Authority* (UKLA), 48 hours prior to the hearing of the application to obtain a listing.

5% test. A test that is applied to establish whether a *Fund* or stakeholder or *Life assurance* product is more like a cash investment (qualifying for the cash component of an *ISA*) or an equity investment (qualifying for the stocks and shares component of an ISA). To qualify for the cash component, a return of at least 95% of the original capital invested must be guaranteed.

'A' Day. 6 April 2006: the date of introduction of 'pensions simplification' – a single tax regime covering all *Registered pension schemes*.

AA. See *Against actual*.

Abandon. The choice made by the holder of an option to allow an option to expire without *Exercise*.

ABS. See *Asset-backed security*.

Absolute advantage. A country has an absolute advantage in the production of a good if it can produce more of the good with a fixed amount of resources than can any other country.

Abstracts. Statements issued by the *Urgent Issues Task Force*. Companies must follow the requirements of Abstracts when preparing their accounts.

Accounting concepts. Basic concepts that underpin accounting and the presentation of the results of an enterprise in its *Financial statements*. Accounting concepts include the *Money measurement concept*, the *Asset measurement concept*, the *Entity concept*, the *Going concern concept*, the *Prudence concept*, the *Consistency concept*, the *Comparability concept*, the *Dual aspect concept* and the Accruals concept (also called the Matching concept).

Accounting equation. The fundamental relationship underlying the *Balance sheet,* which can be expressed as: Assets – Liabilities = Share capital + Reserves.

Accounting standards. Common standards to be followed in accounting and in the presentation of the *Financial statements* of an entity. For a number of years, the *Accounting Standards Board (ASB)* in the UK has been working towards convergence with *International Accounting Standards (IAS)* and *International Financial Reporting Standards (IFRSs)*. Most new standards now issued in the UK mirror their equivalent IAS or IFRS. However, there are still differences between UK *GAAP* and the requirements of IFRSs, as summarised in the following Table.

Topic	UK GAAP	IFRS
Presentation of financial statements	Profit and loss account	Income statement
	Balance sheet totals are net assets and capital and reserves	Balance sheet totals are total assets and capital, reserves and liabilities (or net assets, capital and reserves)
Government grants	CA prohibits netting off of grant against cost of asset	Allows netting off of grant against asset or deferred income method
Construction contracts	Asset split between stocks and debtors in balance sheet	Asset shown totally in receivables
Research and development	May be written off if criteria are met	Must be written off if criteria are met
Investment property	Fair value and no depreciation	Fair value or depreciated cost
	Gains/losses taken to equity	Gains/losses to income statement
Goodwill	Capitalised and amortised over useful life	Capitalised but not amortised – tested for impairment at least annually
Revaluation of non-current assets	Revalued to 'value the business'	Revalued to fair value – usually market value
	Timing of valuations specific	No specification of timings of valuations
Employee benefits	All actuarial gains/losses recognised in equity	Actuarial/gains losses only recognised if exceed a corridor limit and this excess normally amortised over average working lives of employees
Discontinued activities	Shown in columnar or horizontal form in profit and loss account	One line at bottom of income statement
Cash flow statements	Movements in cash only	Movements in cash and cash equivalents
	Eight headings for cash flows	Only three headings for cash flows – operating, investing, financing
Deferred tax	Provided on timing differences	Provided on temporary differences
	Allows discounting	Does not allow discounting

Topic	UK GAAP	IFRS
Associates	Balance sheet – disclose amount of goodwill	No requirement to disclose amount of goodwill
	Profit and loss – show operating profits, exceptional items, interest and tax	Income statement just profit after tax
Joint ventures	Gross equity method	Proportionate consolidation

Accounting Standards Board. The body responsible for issuing *Accounting Standards* in the United Kingdom. See also *Financial Reporting Review Panel*, *Urgent Issues Task Force* and *Financial Reporting Council*.

Accruals. Amounts owed to third parties for which the company has not yet been invoiced. This is shown in the *Balance sheet* of a company as part of *Creditors*. For example, where a company has not been invoiced by a telephone company for its telephone bill for the last three months of the year, it will show in its accounts an accrual for the estimated amount of the bill.

Accruals concept. One of the fundamental *Accounting concepts*, also known as the matching concept. Revenue and costs are credited or charged to the *Profit and loss account* for the year in which they are earned or incurred, not when any cash is received or paid. For example, if a sale is made on credit this year, but the cash is only received next year, the sale is treated as income in this year.

Accumulation units. Units in a *Unit trust* for which the income is reinvested rather than being paid out to as *Dividends*. The reinvested dividends may either increase the unit price, or additional units may be issued.

ACD. See *Authorised Corporate Director*.

Acid test ratio. An accounting ratio usually defined as *Current assets* (with the exception of *Stocks*) divided by *Creditors* falling due within one year. It is designed to test the short-term solvency of a company, in a way similar to the current ratio. Its interpretation is also similar to the *Current ratio*. Also known as the quick ratio.

Acting in concert. For the purpose of the Companies Act 1985 (CA 85), this is when two or more people have an agreement to acquire interests in shares. For the purpose of the *City Code on Takeovers and Mergers*, it is when two or more investors co-operate to obtain or consolidate *Control* of a company.

Active fund management. The approach adopted by fund managers who aim to manage portfolio such that it outperforms the market or a *Benchmark*. The managers aim to achieve outperformance either by selecting specific stocks which they expect to do well, or by timing their purchases of shares, e.g. aiming to buy shares just before the market rises and sell shares just before the market falls (*Market timing*). Fees charged by active fund managers are generally higher than those charged by *Passive fund* managers.

Ad valorem tax. A tax charged as a fixed percentage of the price of a good.

ADP. See *Alternative Delivery Procedure*.

ADR. See *American Depository Receipts (ADRs)*.

Additional Voluntary Contributions (AVCs). A facility through which members of an *Occupational pension scheme* (OPS) can choose to make further retirement provision. The arrangement may be 'in-house' – i.e. part of the OPS itself, or it may be 'free-standing' – i.e. independent of the main scheme.

Against actual. A term used for an *Exchange for Physical (EFP)*.

Agency broker. A broker who only acts as *Agent* (on behalf of a customer) and does not deal as *Principal* or as *Market maker*.

Agency cross. A trade between two customers of a *Broker* executed through the office of the broker who acts as *Agent* in the middle, with the two customers acting as *Principals*. It will usually be carried out at the mid-market price for the stock in question. The broker will charge both customers commission.

Agent. A person, acting on behalf of somebody else, who is the *Principal* to the trade when completing the trade. An example is when a *Broker-dealer* buys or sells shares on behalf of a customer with a *Market maker*.

Aggregate demand. The total demand for goods and services in an economy.

Aggregate supply. The total supply of goods and services in an economy.

Aggregation service. A service that allows the user to track the value of all their financial accounts and assets, even if they are held with a range of financial institutions, through a single secure online site using a single user name and password.

AGM. See *Annual General Meeting*.

AIM. See *Alternative Investment Market*.

Allocation. Often, in *Open outcry* markets the trader who has effected a bargain is not the owner of the trade, having initiated it on behalf of another firm. Allocation refers to the process of allocating, or 'giving up' the trade within the *Trade Registration System (TRS)* to the originating firm, so that the trade ends up in the appropriate firm's account.

Alpha. A measure of the risk-adjusted return of a security or of a *Fund*. Alpha measures the difference between the actual return and its expected performance, given its level of *Risk* as measured by its *Beta*. A positive alpha indicates that the investment has performed better than expected, given its level of risk (beta). A negative alpha indicates that the investment has underperformed for a security or fund with its level of risk. In practice, for funds, a negative alpha is more likely because of the effect of fund management charges in reducing the overall return. Many *Hedge funds* claim to create 'positive alpha' by making positive returns compared with risk they have taken on.

Alternative delivery procedure (ADP). Relating to *Futures*, where the long and short sides of a transaction agree to deliver either a different specification of the product from that stipulated in the contract specification, or to a different location from those included in the contract specification, or both. ADPs are not covered by the London Clearing House guarantee.

Alternative Investment Market (AIM). A market for issuing and trading shares operated by the *London Stock Exchange*. The AIM is designed to be a lightly regulated market with low regulatory costs for companies, while giving the company the ability to raise capital and investors the ability to trade their shares. The AIM is potentially attractive for smaller companies for whom an official listing would be both expensive and cumbersome. As the AIM is a more lightly regulated market, and AIM companies may be relatively small and may have only a short trading record, the AIM involves increased risk for investors than the listed companies market.

Alternatively Secured Pension (ASP). Income secured from a pension scheme in such a way as to avoid the need to purchase an annuity by age 75. The ASP is intended to provide for members of certain religious groups, for whom the pooled mortality basis of annuities is not acceptable.

American Depository Receipts (ADRs). Certificates issued in the USA representing the right to ownership of shares in a UK (or other foreign) company. A bank will buy shares in a UK company and issue receipts into the US in respect of those shares. For example, one ADR might represent the right to eight or ten shares in a company. The ADR will trade in USA dollars. The bank will receive payment of dividends in *Sterling*, but will convert them to dollars to pay to ADR holders. ADR holders have the right to vote but are not allowed to participate in rights issues. ADRs provide for US investors a convenient way to invest in UK or other foreign companies. *Global Depository Receipts (GDRs)* and *International Depository Receipts (IDRs)* operate worldwide on the same basis. See also *Crest Depository Interests (CDIs)*.

American-style option. An *Option* where the holder has the right to *Exercise* up to and including the *Expiry* date. Contrast with a *European style option*, where the holder has the right to exercise the option on the expiry date only.

AML (Anti-Money Laundering). The legal controls requiring financial and other institutions to seek to prevent, or to report, *Money laundering* activities.

AMPS. See *Auction market preferred stock*.

Ancillary services. In the *MiFID* framework, the following 'non-core' services in respect of which investment firms are regulated: safekeeping and administration of financial instruments including custodianship, collateral and cash management; granting credit or loans to an investor to enable him to carry out a transaction in which the firm is involved; advising undertakings on capital structure or industrial strategy; advising on mergers and acquisitions; foreign exchange services connected with providing investment services; investment research; financial analysis or other general recommendations relating to transactions in financial instruments.

Annual General Meeting (AGM). All companies are required to hold an AGM at least once every 15 months. However, the AGM must be held every calendar year. Shareholders must be given 21 calendar days' notice of the meeting and this may only be waived if all the shareholders agree.

Annual report and accounts. All limited companies are required by law to prepare an annual report each year, containing their *Financial statements*, directors' report and auditor report. The annual report of a listed company may also contain a five-year summary of results. The annual report must be sent to shareholders and to the Registrar of Companies, a Government agency whose role it is to maintain records of companies. Once sent to the Registrar, the annual report becomes a public document, available for anyone to view.

Annuity. An equal annual cash flow for a set period of time. In the context of life company products, an annuity can be purchased for a lump sum – for example, from a pension arrangement – to provide an income until the annuitant dies, and sometimes for a guaranteed period even if the annuitant dies during the period.

Appointed representative. Businesses or self-employed individuals who act on behalf of a firm through an agency contract for services. In certain markets, e.g. *Life assurance*, the bulk of sales take place through appointed representatives. An appointed representative generally carries out *Regulated activities* but is exempt from the need to seek authorisation. The responsibility to control appointed representatives is borne by an *Authorised firm*. The exemption removes them from the scope of authorisation so long as they usually act solely on behalf of one authorised firm and have a contract with that firm setting out the scope of the appointment and any requirements imposed by the authorised firm. Under the *Markets in Financial Instruments Directive (MiFID)*, an appointed representative is known as a *Tied agent*.

Appropriate examinations. 'Appropriate examination' requirements apply to *Designated investment business* carried on for a *Retail client*, except that they do not apply to providing basic advice on non-deposit-based *Stakeholder products*, and to regulated *Mortgage* activity and home reversion schemes. Employees must not carry out these activities without first passing the relevant regulatory module of an appropriate examination. The *Financial Services Authority (FSA)* maintains a list of appropriate examinations for the activities for which they are required, from which firms may choose. Although a firm may set its own examinations, choosing examinations from the FSA list may be relied on as 'tending to establish compliance' with the *T&C* rules. Firms may choose to impose time limits on the time by which examinations must be passed, or on the number of times examinations can be attempted.

Appropriate Personal Pension (APP). A personal pension plan which can accept Protected Rights (contracted-out) contributions.

Appropriateness rules. Rules applying to a firm providing investment services in the course of *MiFID business*, other than making a personal recommendation and managing investments. The rules thus generally apply to *Execution-only* services which are available in the UK, where transactions are undertaken at the initiative of the customer without advice having been given. *Suitability rules* apply where there is a personal recommendation.) One firm may rely on another *MiFID* firm's assessment of appropriateness, in line with the general rule on reliance on other investment firms. To assess appropriateness, the firm must ask the client to provide information on his knowledge and experience in the relevant investment field, to enable the assessment to be made.

Approved person. Someone who has shown they are fit and proper, for the purpose of performing a controlled function in an *FSA* firm.

Arbitrage. The purchase (or sale) of an instrument and the simultaneous taking of an equal and opposite position in a related instrument to exploit a mispricing. See *Arbitrageur*.

Arbitrage channel. An area that exists both above and below the fair value of a future, within which no arbitrage will take place. This is because additional costs, such as exchange fees, bid offer spreads and commissions, will exceed *Arbitrage* profits within this channel. Thus, the width of the channel depends on the costs incurred by the participant in the market place.

Arbitrageur. Someone who trades in the markets with the intention of making riskless, guaranteed profits by exploiting market inefficiencies. For example, if the same index contract is traded in two different exchanges, it should trade at the same price in both exchanges. If the prices are not the same, an arbitrageur will buy at the cheaper price and immediately sell at the more expensive price in the other market, making a guaranteed profit.

Arithmetic mean. The simple average that is calculated by adding up the observed values and dividing by the number of observed items.

ARROW. A system developed by the *FSA's* as part of its overall 'risk-based' approach to supervision. ARROW – the **A**dvanced **R**isk **R**esponsive **O**perating Frame**W**ork – involves the FSA examining particular risks posed by individual firms and also risks to consumers and to the industry as a whole. ARROW II is a revised model introduced in 2006 which is designed to allow FSA supervisors more accurately to reflect their assessment of risk in individual firms or through cross-firm 'thematic' work.

Articles of Association. The document that acts as a contract between a company and its shareholders, outlining the rights and duties of the shareholders with the company and between themselves. See also *Memorandum of Association* – the other main constitutional document of a company.

Asian-style option. An *Option* that is exercised at the average underlying price over a period.

Asking price. The market selling price. See *Offer price*.

Asset allocation. The stage where the investment manager decides what proportion of the total portfolio to invest in broad asset categories, such as shares, *Bonds*, *Property* and cash.

Asset measurement concept. The concept in accounting which dictates that (1) monetary assets (such as amounts owed, or cash balances at the bank) should be reflected in the accounts of the enterprise at their *Fair* value, while (2) non-monetary assets (for example, cars or inventories of manufactured product) should, on the other hand, generally be recorded at an amount based on their cost.

Asset swap. When the interest streams being exchanged through an *Interest rate swap* are funded with interest received on specific assets, the swap is called an asset swap. Asset swaps may also be *Coupon swaps* or *Basis swaps*.

Asset-backed security (ABS). A financial security that is collateralised (backed) by asset which may include *Bonds*, loan repayments, leases, *Receivables* or *Property*.

Assets. Resources owned and controlled by a company, technically defined as access, t future economic benefits as a result of past events or transactions. Assets are shown on company's *Balance sheet*.

Assets Recovery Agency (ARA). A Government agency set up under the *Proceeds of Crime Act 2002* in order to confiscate the proceeds of crime from criminals.

Assignment. (1) The process whereby, when an *Option* is exercised by the holder, the clearing house will randomly match the exercise notice received against an open *Short position*, and advise the chosen *Writer* of the requirement to fulfil his contractual obligation (2) The process by which a trade is directed into the appropriate account in the *Trade Registration System*, into the house, segregated or non-segregated account of the firm.

Association of Investment Companies (AIC). An association that represents *Investment trusts*.

At-the-money. A feature of an *Option or Warrant* when the *Exercise price* is equal to the current market price of the asset, subject to the option. For example, a *Call option* with an exercise price of 100p on a share with a share price of 100p is at-the-money. More generally, however, an at-the-money option is an option whose exercise price is nearest to that of the *Underlying asset*. For example, where an option has strike prices at intervals of 10p, e.g. 90p, 100p, 110p etc, if the underlying asset has a price of 97p, the at-the-money option is said to be the 100p strike, which is the nearest *Strike price* to the underlying price. See also *In-the-money* and *Out-of-the-money*.

Auction. A common method of issuing *Gilts*. Similar to a *Tender offer*. In an auction, investors apply to buy the new gilts being issued, specifying the amount they wish to purchase and the price they are prepared to pay. The new gilts will be issued to investors who bid the highest prices and investors pay the price that they bid. This is the one difference between the auction and the tender: in a tender, investors all pay the same *Strike price*, regardless of what price they bid.

Auction market preferred stock (AMPS). *Preference shares* issued by a company where the *Dividend* is variable and is set at regular intervals to a market rate by means of an *Auction* process between investors.

Audit. See *Internal audit* and *External audit*.

Audit committee. A committee establishing processes and procedures and creating monitoring to ensure all processes and procedures across the financial institution are followed. The audit committee typically acts independently of management and has oversight responsibilities. In some jurisdictions, institutions are required to have an independent audit committee made up entirely of outside directors, independent of management. They are charged with reviewing the policies, procedures and financial reports with management and the independent accountants. Certain country regulations require audit committees to possess both banking and management expertise to offer the best guidance and oversight to the organisation.

Audit trail. The range of documents and other evidence which records all business activities and transactions that the firm effects. Such a historic record allows the firm to piece together the chronology of a trade. It is also required for compliance purposes.

Auditor's Report. All companies above a certain size are required to have their financial statements audited, i.e. checked for truth and fairness, by a registered external auditor. The auditor prepares a report, which is attached to the *Financial statements*, stating his opinion as to whether or not the financial statements give a true and fair view of the company's affairs.

AUT. An FSA-authorised *Unit Trust*.

Authorised Corporate Director (ACD).The person responsible for the day-to-day management of the assets within an *Open-Ended Investment Company (OEIC)*.

Authorised firm. The process by which organisations are vetted and licensed to conduct investment business (specifically, '*Regulated activities*') under the *Financial Services and Markets Act 2000* is called 'authorisation' and such organisations are known as authorised firms. The process of authorisation is sometimes referred to as 'Part IV Permission'.

Automatic exercise. A procedure whereby clearing houses exercise all manifestly *In-the-money Options* at *Expiry* without requiring instructions (in the form of an *Exercise* notice) from the holder. Most automatic exercise routines will not exercise options that are only just in-the-money.

Automatic matching. The process of instantly matching orders entered onto electronic dealing systems, such as *SETS* and *LIFFE CONNECT®*.

AVCs. See *Additional Voluntary Contributions*.

Average cost. For a given level of output, the total cost divided by the total quantity produced.

Backwardation. (1) A situation in which the *Bid price* exceeds the *Offer price* for a stock – for example, where the prices are 512-510. This means that the best price at which *Market makers* will sell the stock is less than the best price at which they will buy the stock. This is unusual, since market makers will normally want to operate with a spread, buying stocks for less than the price at which they will sell them. The reason for backwardation is usually some market distortion, such as a share repurchase scheme by the company. When the price is backward, the touch strip on the *SEAQ* screen turns red. See also *Choice price*. (2) In *Futures* markets, a situation in which the future price is less than the cash price. See also *Contango*.

Bad delivery. A situation where the *Registrar* rejects a request to transfer ownership, so the transfer is not registered.

Balance of payments. The statement that summarises cash inflows and outflows between a country and the rest of the world as a result of imports, exports and capital investment. See also *Current account* and *Capital account*.

Balance sheet. A statement of the financial position of an enterprise at a given point in time. The balance sheet details the assets of the company and how these assets are being financed. The balance sheet is based on the equivalence of (1) *Net assets* and (2) *Shareholders' funds* (financing).

Balloon maturity. A situation where a large amount of the principal relating to a *Bond* issue reaches *Maturity* in a single year.

Bancassurance. The selling of assurance products by banks.

Bank of England. The UK's *Central bank*, with responsibility for the setting of *Interest rates* through its *Monetary Policy Committee (MPC)*. It is the *Lender of last resort* to prevent a systemic collapse in the banking system. The Bank of England Registrar maintains the *Register* of ownership of *Gilts*.

Banking Code. A voluntary code to which most banks and *Building societies* subscribe and which sets standards of good banking practice for the institutions to follow when dealing with personal customers in the UK.

Banking Consolidation Directive (BCD). A *European Union* Directive of 2001 which updated various earlier banking Directives and provides the rights of *Credit institutions* in respect of *Passporting*.

Bankruptcy Restriction Order (BRO). A Court Order, lasting for between 2 and 15 years, and designed to protect the public from a bankrupt whose conduct has been irresponsible or reckless.

Barrier to entry. A factor which makes it difficult for suppliers to enter a market.

Base requirement. The amount of capital required for an *FSA* firm to cover its operating costs in periods of low activity.

Basel Capital Accord. An Accord of the *Basel Committee on Banking Supervision*, implemented in 1988, which aimed for a standardised strategy for measuring certain risks, such as *Credit risk*, for credit institutions. Most countries with active international banks have applied this framework. A revised Accord, referred to as *'Basel II'* and with the full formal title *'International convergence of capital measurement and capital standards – a revised framework'*, is reflected in EU law via the *Capital Requirements Directive*.

Basel Committee on Banking Supervision. The Basel Committee was established by various *Central banks* in 1974. The Committee's members come from some of the major financial centres such as the UK and US. Countries are represented by their central bank (e.g. the *Bank of England*) and, if different, also by their prudential supervisory authority (e.g. the *FSA*). The Committee meets four times a year and has various working groups and task forces which also meet regularly. It does not have legal powers but creates common standards and guidelines of best practice with the aim that individual states will implement these in their own law. The Committee has tried to reduce divergences in international supervisory standards. It seeks to ensure that all foreign banking establishments are actually supervised by someone and that supervision is adequate. To achieve this, the Committee has issued a large number of policies and recommendations.

Basel II. The second of the Accords of the *Basel Committee on Banking Supervision*. Basel II is a revision of the previously existing prudential framework and has the following aspects: increased sensitivity to the risks that firms face, with an explicit measure for operational risk and risk weightings against *Credit risk*; introduction of the internal ratings based approach (IRB) which allows firms to rely to some extent on their own credit risk estimates; incentives for firms to improve their risk management practices. The new framework aims to leave the overall level of capital held by banks collectively broadly unchanged.

Basis. The difference between the price of a *Futures* contract and that of the *Underlying asset*. Calculated by subtracting the futures price from the cash price.

Basis point (bp). One-hundredth of one per cent (0.01%), for example in relation to *Interest rate* changes.

Basis risk. The basis for a particular product does not necessarily stay constant and changes in basis can occur for a variety of reasons. Such changes can cause either a profit or loss to be incurred by the holder of the product and thus constitute a *Risk*. Basis risk can mean that a person using *Futures* to hedge an underlying cash position cannot obtain a perfect *Hedge* where profits on one side of the hedge exactly offset losses on the other.

Basis trading. The simultaneous entry into both a cash position for a particular product and an equal and opposite *Futures* position on the same *Underlying*. A basis trader looks to profit from a change in the relationship between the cash price and the future, i.e. from a change in the *Basis*.

Basis Trading Facility (BTF). A system operated on the *Euronext.liffe* market for certain *Bond* futures that allows for the simultaneous execution of cash and futures trades (*Basis trading*).

Basis swap. An arrangement to swap two interest streams which are both calculated using *Floating interest rates*, e.g. three-month *LIBOR* versus six-month *LIBOR*.

BCD. See *Banking Consolidation Directive*.

Bear. A person expecting a general decline in prices, especially share prices – in contrast to a *Bull*.

Bear spread. An example of a *Vertical spread*, constructed by the purchase of a high strike call (put) and the sale of a low strike call (put), both options being on the same *Underlying asset* and having the same delivery month. Entered into when moderately bearish.

Bearer securities. An instrument for which there is no register of the owner held by the issuer. Evidence of ownership is given by physical possession of the instrument itself. Bearer stock is common in the *Eurobond* market. Contrasts with *Registered securities*.

Benchmark. A standard, for example an index, used for comparison, especially to assess how well a fund manager performs. We can determine whether the fund manager has outperformed, matched, or underperformed that benchmark. The appropriate benchmark is one that is consistent with the preferences of the fund's trustees and the fund's tax status.

BERR. See *Department for Business, Enterprise and Regulatory Reform*.

Best execution. The basic *COBS* rule, applying to both *Retail* and *Professional clients* and stated as follows: 'A firm must take all reasonable steps to obtain, when executing orders, the best possible result for its clients taking into account the execution factors'. The obligation to obtain best execution needs to be interpreted according to the particular type of financial instrument involved, but the rule applies to all types of financial instrument. The 'best possible result' must be determined in terms of total consideration – taking into account any costs, including the firm's own commissions in the case of competing execution venues, and not just quoted prices. However, the firm is not expected to compare the result with that of clients of other firms. Commissions structure must not discriminate between execution venues.

Beta (β) (or beta factor). A relative measure of the *Systematic risk* of an investment. The sign of the beta (+/-) indicates whether, on average, the investment's returns move with (+) the market, rising and falling when it does, or in the opposite direction (−) to the market. The value of the beta indicates the relative *Volatility* (see box below).

Beta factors

$\beta = 1$	A security with a beta of 1 moves in line with the market. If the market (e.g., as indicated by a share price index such as the *FTSE 100 Index*) moves up 5%, the price of this security is likely to move up 5%.
$\beta > 1$ If	A security with a beta factor greater than 1 varies more widely than the market. the market moves up 5%, the price of a security with a beta of 2 is likely to move up 10%.
$\beta < 1$	A security with a beta factor of less than 1 fluctuates less than the wider market. If the market moves up or down 10%, the price of a security with a beta of 0.5 is likely to move up or down respectively by 5%.

Bid offer spread (or bid ask spread). The quantitative difference between the *Bid price* and the *Offer price* of a security.

Bid price. The price at which a *Market maker* is bidding to buy shares. The bid price generally lower than the *Offer price* at which the market maker will sell shares. For example, a quote of 54-56 indicates a bid price of 54p and an offer price of 56p.

BIFFEX. The Baltic International Freight Futures Exchange.

Big Bang. A term used for the changes taking effect on 27 October 1986, when the system of share trading in the UK was radically changed to remove fixed commissions and to introduce screen-based trading.

Black Monday. A name given to the date 19 October 1987, when there was a major worldwide stock market crash.

Black-Scholes model. A theoretical *Option* pricing model which is in widespread use in the market place, named after Fischer Black and Myron Scholes who developed the model.

Block trade. Trading in a large quantity of securities, normally by institutional investors. Defined on the *LSE* as at least 75 × *Normal Market Size (NMS)* for securities with NMS of 2,000 shares or more, and 50 x NMS for a security with an NMS of 1,000. The term also refers to privately negotiated *Futures* transactions executed separately from the public *Auction* market. Display of such larger trades is usually delayed for up to five business days. Block trading is often referred to as *Upstairs trading* in the US.

Blue Book. See *City Code on Takeovers and Mergers*.

Blue chip. A phrase used to describe shares of the highest quality and lowest risk.

BOAT. Project BOAT led to the creation of Markit BOAT™, a price-reporting and display platform set up by a consortium of European banks to take advantage of *MiFID* by competing with exchange-based price display facilities. BOAT enables investment firms to meet their pre-trade quoting and post-trade reporting obligations for all European OTC equity trades. The platform collects, collates, validates and stores OTC trade data and publishes it to the market in real-time. With the support of over 22 investment houses, BOAT has the ability to capture and publish a majority of the daily volume of OTC trades in the *EEA*.

Bobl. Medium-term German Government debt.

Bond. A certificate indicating ownership of debt, giving details of the key terms of the underlying loan. Bonds are usually tradeable. The asset class of fixed interest securities is often generally referred to as bonds. See also *Debenture*.

Bond washing. The process of selling a *Bond Cum-dividend* and then repurchasing it when it is *Ex-dividend*, so as to convert the *Coupon* element of the bond's price into a capital gain rather than receiving the coupon as income. This does not, however, affect the investor's UK tax liability since the element of the gain on sale due to the interest accrual in the bond's price is taxed as income.

Bonus issue. Also known as a scrip issue, a capitalisation issue, a free issue or a gratis issue, it is the issue of new fully paid shares in a company to existing shareholders for free on a basis *pro rata* to existing holdings. For example, a 1 for 4 bonus issue would mean that a shareholder would receive one free share for every four existing shares they own in the company. The impact of a bonus issue is to reduce the share price, since the same total market capitalisation is being spread over a larger number of shares. This may have a beneficial impact in terms of liquidity of trading.

Book entry system. An electronic system of keeping records of ownership of shares and bonds so that all records are computerised. In the UK, the major example of a book entry system is *CREST*.

Book value. (1) The value at which a loan is shown in the *Balance sheet* of the company that has borrowed the money. The book value is not necessarily the market value of the loan. (2) Generally, the value at which an asset is shown in books of account.

Bookbuilding. A method of implementing an *Offer for subscription* or an *Offer for sale*. It is a compromise method of issue that draws on elements of a fixed price offer and a *Tender*. Prior to the issue of shares, the issuing house conducts a bookbuilding exercise where it contacts investors and obtains commitments to purchase a number of shares at a specified price. Having established the demand for the shares over a two-week period or so, the issuing manager sets the fixed price for the issue in line with the demand levels that have been established. Bookbuilding is a common method of implementing very large offers where the level of the issue price is difficult to determine in advance and where it is difficult to obtain an *Underwriter* for the issue.

Books closed date. See *Record date*.

Borrowing. In relation to *Futures* trading on the *LME*, the buying of near-dated contracts and the selling of long-dated contracts – an example of a 'carry'. The equivalent of an intra-market spread trade, sometimes known as 'buying the spread'. See also *Carrying* and *Intra-market spread*.

Bought deal. A means of issuing *Eurobonds*. The lead manager of the issuer buys the whole issue on predetermined terms and price and then places the bonds with its own clients. See also *Fixed price re-offer*.

Breakeven point. The underlying price at which a strategy is neither profitable nor unprofitable.

Bridge. The electronic link between *Euroclear* and *Clearstream*, the two *Eurobond* clearing houses.

British Bankers Association (BBA). An association acting on behalf of its 260 members, who are banks operating in the UK, on domestic and international issues.

Broker. A person who acts as an intermediary between two other persons, enabling them to complete a trade together.

Broker-dealer. A member of the Stock Exchange who may trade with customers either as *Principal* or act as *Agent* on their behalf, completing a trade for the customer with a *Market maker* or doing an *Agency cross*. See also *Dual capacity*.

Brokerage. Commission charges payable on securities transactions.

BTAN. Bons à Taux Annuel Normalisé. Medium-term French Government debt.

BTF. See *Basis Trading Facility*.

Building society. A form of mutual organisation owned by its depositors and borrowers. Building societies' original purpose was to take deposits and recycle these as *Mortgage* loans for buying houses. However, modern larger building societies have extended their role such that they are now similar to retail banks in many ways. Building societies are permitted to raise 50 per cent of funds through the wholesale market.

Bull. Someone expecting a general rise in prices, especially share prices – in contrast to a *Bear*.

Bulldog bond. A *Sterling* bond issued in the United Kingdom by a foreign issuer.

Bullet form (or bullet maturity). A form of debt issue where the capital is all redeemed on the final day of the life of the *Bond*, rather than in instalments over the life. The only payments over the life of the bond are the *Coupon*.

Bund. Long-term German Government bond.

Business risk. The risk of loss due to an adverse external environment such as high *Inflation* affecting labour costs, an over-competitive market reducing margins, or legal, tax or regulatory changes.

Business Order. In financial services regulation, the name often used for the (Carrying on Regulated Activities By Way of Business) Order 2001, as amended, through which *HM Treasury* is given the power to specify circumstances in which an activity is not carried on by way of business .

Business risk. The uncertainty of cash flows generated by the firm's business.

Bull spread. In relation to *Options*, an example of a *Vertical spread*, constructed by the purchase of a low strike call (put) and the sale of a high strike call (put), both options being on the same *Underlying* and having the same delivery month. Entered into when moderately bullish.

Cabinet trade. Sometimes used as an alternative to the simple abandonment of a long *Options* position. This is where a worthless position is closed (sold) for a notional consideration in order to facilitate the crystallisation of losses for taxation and accounting purposes.

Cable. A term used to refer to the *Sterling*/US dollar exchange rate.

CAC 40. The major French share price index, comprising the top 40 listed shares.

CAD. See *Capital Adequacy Directive*.

Calendar spread. See *Horizontal spread*.

Call option. An option that gives the holder (the buyer of the option) the right, but not the obligation, to buy (call) an asset at a given price, on or before a given date.

Call warrant. See *Covered warrant*.

Cap. In the context of *CREST*, a member's credit limit with his payment bank. The payment bank guarantees to meet client obligations up to this maximum.

Capital account. The part of the *Balance of payments* which is due to transactions in long-term assets and liabilities, such as when a UK company acquires an overseas subsidiary.

Capital adequacy. The measure of the sufficiency of a firm's funds to meet its business and regulatory obligations. See also *Financial resources*.

Capital Adequacy Directive (CAD). An EU Directive aiming to create a harmonised set of capital requirements for *Credit institutions* and *Investment firms*.

Capital allowances. The form of 'tax depreciation' charged against profits when calculating taxable profits for *Corporation tax* purposes, as opposed to the *Depreciation* charge in a company's accounts. Accounting depreciation is not allowed as a deduction from profits in calculating the corporation tax liability since there is too much discretion in the amount of depreciation that a company may charge in its accounts. As a result, the capital allowances calculation is defined precisely in law.

Capital Asset Pricing Model (CAPM). A theoretical model suggesting that, for any given level of risk in relation to the market portfolio, an investor can achieve an expected return by investing in some combination of stock market and risk-free investments. CAPM assumes that investors are rational, risk-averse and well diversified. All investors are assumed to have the same expectations, and there exists a risk-free rate at which all investors may borrow or lend without limit.

Capital employed. The underlying asset base a company needs to generate its profits and revenue. Usually defined for a business as *Non-current assets* plus *Working capital*, although alternative definitions are possible. Capital employed can also be calculated by adding together *Shareholders' funds* and long-term liabilities.

Capital gearing ratio. The proportion of a company's capital that is borrowed, expressed as:

$$\frac{\text{Prior charge capital}}{\text{Total capital}}$$

Capital Requirements Directive (CRD). An EU Directive which introduces a supervisory framework reflecting the *Basel II* rules on capital measurement and capital standards. The CRD amends two existing Directives: the *Capital Adequacy Directive (CAD)* and the *Banking Consolidation Directive (BCD)*.

Capitalisation issue. See *Bonus issue*.

CAPM. See *Capital Asset Pricing Model*.

Carbon trading (or emissions trading). A 'cap and trade' system of economic incentives that aims to achieve reductions in the emission of 'greenhouse' gases and other pollutants. Caps are set on permitted levels of emissions by a central government or other authority. Emission permits are issued to companies and other entities, who are required to hold the equivalent number of credits which give the right to make specific levels of emissions. Companies wishing to emit more must buy credits from those companies who pollute less. Those who can reduce emissions at lowest cost will tend to do so under this system, and this should lead to reduction in pollution at the lowest cost. The *European Union* operates an Emission Trading Scheme, and in the US there is a national market to reduce acid rain as well as regional markets for nitrous oxide.

Carrying (Carries). On the *LME*, carrying describes the borrowing or lending activity. Another term for an *Intra-market spread*.

Cash Against Documents (CAD). An alternative term for *Delivery versus payment (DvP)*.

Cash and carry arbitrage. An arbitrage trade entered into where a *Futures* contract is sold and the *Underlying asset* is purchased in the cash market. Such a trade will be effected where the trader believes that the futures are trading relatively expensive to their Fair value.

Cash flow statement. Part of a company's financial statements, being a summary of all the cash flows of the company over a period of time, usually one year, broken down into various categories.

Cash market. The market place for the immediate delivery of and payment for assets.

Cash Memorandum Account (CMA). The record of each *CREST member's* payment obligations. These accounts do not represent cash, but rather obligations of members payment banks to transfer funds at the end of the day.

Cash settlement. (1) The settlement on the business day following the day of the trade – normal settlement for *Gilts* and new issues. (2) In respect of *Derivatives*, the settlement of *Futures* and *Options* contracts for cash instead of settlement involving the physical transfer of goods – typically used for index-based products such as the FTSE 100 Index future and option.

CASS. The Client Assets rules, found in the *FSA Handbook*.

CBOE. See *Chicago Board Options Exchange*. One of the largest options exchanges in the world. CBOE has set up CBOE Stock Exchange (CBSX) for *Equities* trading. There is also a CBOE Futures Exchange.

CBOT. See *Chicago Board of Trade*.

CCSS. See *CREST Courier and Sorting Service*.

CD. See *Certificate of Deposit*.

CDO. See *Collateralised debt obligation*.

CDS. See *Credit default swap*.

Central bank. A bank that is responsible for control of the credit system, sometimes under instruction from government or, increasingly, under its own authority. The *Bank of England* is the UK's central bank. The central bank acts as banker to banks, and as *Lender of last resort*.

Central Counterparty Clearing (CCC). A process by which equities transactions are cleared by a single ('central') counterparty. Widespread adoption of the central counterparty approach is relatively recent. Potential advantages are enhanced trading liquidity, reduction of risk and improved operational efficiency.

Central Securities Depository (CSD). A *Depository* for holding securities in the domestic market. Almost all countries have some form of central depository where the securities are either immobilised or dematerialised. Efficiency gains are achieved through the elimination of manual errors, lower costs and increased speed of processing through automation, which all translate into lower risks. In a 'dematerialised' system, there is no document which physically embodies the claim. The system relies on a collection of securities accounts, instructions to financial institutions which maintain those accounts, and confirmations of account entries.

Certificate of Deposit (CD). A type of money market instrument. The certificate is evidence of a deposit made with a bank, which will be redeemed on the maturity date with interest. The difference between a Certificate of Deposit and a normal deposit with a bank is that a Certificate of Deposit is a bearer instrument that can be sold on in the *Money markets* to another investor.

Certification. The process of authorising a *Stock transfer form* to be deposited and registered without the cover of a certificate. It can only be carried out by the *Registrar*. Certification may be required if: (1) one certificate is used to cover more than one trade, (2) stock recently purchased is being sold, yet the original certificate has not yet been received, (3) a balancing certificate requested due to previous trade has not been received and that stock is now being sold.

Ceteris paribus. The assumption that all other things remain equal.

CFA Institute. (Formerly the Association for Investment Management and Research.) A membership organisation that awards the Chartered Financial Analyst® (CFA®) designation and sets standards of ethics and professional excellence.

Chargeable accounting period. A company calculates its profits for its chargeable accounting period and then pays *Corporation tax* on these profits. The chargeable accounting period is normally the same period of time as the company's accounting year. However, a chargeable accounting period cannot be for longer than one year. If a company changes its accounting year end, for example from 31 March to 30 June, in the year of the change, it will have a 15-month accounting period, from 1 April one year to 30 June the next year. For tax purposes, it will be obliged to break this down into two chargeable accounting periods, one of 12 months and one of three months.

Chargeable disposal. A disposal of an asset for capital gains tax purposes. This will include the sale of an asset, the gift of an asset or an asset becoming worthless, such as shares when a company becomes insolvent.

Chargeable estate. The amount of an individual's estate that is liable to *Inheritance tax*.

Charge. The situation arising when a *Bond* is issued with *Security* over certain assets. If the borrower defaults on the bond, the charged assets can be sold and the proceeds used to repay the debt to the lender. A fixed charge is a charge over a specific asset, usually land and buildings, in which case it is also known as a *Mortgage*. A floating charge is a charge over a class of assets, such as the stock in trade of the business. Bonds issued with a fixed charge are often known as debenture stock.

Charterparty. A legal document produced when an agreement to charter a ship is made on the Baltic Exchange, setting out all the terms and conditions for the voyage to be undertaken.

Chartism. See *Technical analysis*.

Cheapest to deliver (CTD). All bond *Futures* have a range of deliverable bonds that underlie the futures contract, giving the seller the choice as to which one he delivers to meet his contractual obligations. The deliverable bond that generates for the seller the greatest profit or the least loss on a bond futures position is the cheapest to deliver, and can be identified by calculating the returns from a cash and carry *Arbitrage* on each of the deliverable bonds. The bond that gives the greatest arbitrage profit, or the least arbitrage loss, is the cheapest to deliver.

Chicago Board of Trade (CBOT). Established in 1848, it is the world's oldest *Derivatives* (futures and futures-options) exchange. More than 3,600 CBOT members trade 53 different futures and options products at the CBOT, resulting in an annual trading volume for 2003 of more than 454 million contracts. The CBOT's principal role is to provide contract markets for its members and customers and to oversee the integrity and cultivation of those markets. Its markets provide prices that result from trading in open auction or electronic platforms. The marketplace assimilates new information throughout the trading day, and through trading it translates this information into *Benchmark* prices agreed upon by buyers and sellers. In 2007, CBOT completed a merger with the *Chicago Mercantile Exchange*, forming the *CME Group*.

Chicago Board Options Exchange (CBOE). One of the largest options exchanges in the world. CBOE has set up *CBOE Stock Exchange (CBSX)* for equities trading. There is also a CBOE Futures Exchange (CBE).

Chicago Mercantile Exchange (CME). The Chicago Mercantile Exchange (CME or 'The Merc') was founded in 1898, demutualised in November 2000 and went public in December 2002. In 2007, CME completed a merger with the *Chicago Board of Trade*, forming the *CME Group*. CME trades *Interest rates*, *Equities*, currencies, and *Commodities* and also offers trading in alternative investments such as *Real estate* and weather derivatives. CME has the highest open interest (number of contracts outstanding) options and futures contracts of any futures exchange globally. Trading is conducted both by *Open outcry* and (around 70 per cent) on the CME Globex® electronic trading platform.

Child Trust Fund (CTF). A tax-free account available for a child born on or after 1 September 2002 and offered by banks, *Building societies* and other providers. The government makes initial contributions and friends or family of the child may contribute more, within limits. The child receives the funds on becoming 18.

Chinese walls. Physical/procedural barriers erected to prevent the flow of information within a firm, e.g. between corporate finance and investment management. Under *FSA* rules, it is not obligatory to establish Chinese walls.

Chi-X. Instinet's Chi-X is an order-driven pan-European matching engine and central limit order book or *MTF* aiming to provide clients with a fast, cheap and high-capacity alternative to trading on-exchange.

Choice price. A situation in which the touch *Bid* and *Offer prices* for a stock are the same. The touch strip on the *SEAQ* screen will remain yellow. See also *Backwardation*.

Churning. The act of a firm or adviser engaging in excessive trading to generate commission. Churning and *Switching* contravene the *Client's best interests rule*. Churning relates to investments generally, while *Switching* describes overtrading within and between *Packaged products*.

CINS. An acronym for CUSIP International Numbering System. See *CUSIP*.

Circus swap. A swap made up of a cross-currency *Coupon swap* (fixed against floating) and a single-currency coupon swap. The purpose is to synthesise either a pure fixed against fixed currency swap or a cross-currency *Basis swap*.

City Code. The City Code on Takeovers and Mergers, alternatively known as the Takeover Code or the 'Blue Book'. The Code comprises the principles and rules of the *Takeover Panel* governing takeovers and mergers of public companies and certain private companies. The City Code applies to all offers for public companies which have their registered offices in the United Kingdom, the Channel Islands or the Isle of Man if any of their securities are admitted to trading on a regulated market in the United Kingdom (*UK RIE*) or on any stock exchange in the Channel Islands or the Isle of Man, or if they have their place of central management and control in the United Kingdom, the Channel Islands or the Isle of Man.

Civil offence. The aim of the civil law is to compensate victims (although the *Market abuse* offence also provides for punishment via fines). A civil offence is punishable in either the County Court or High Court. Penalties include making contracts voidable, damages, compensation / restitutions orders and injunctions. The burden of proof is 'the balance of probabilities', unlike the 'beyond reasonable doubt' test for a *Criminal offence*.

Civil partnership. A form of legal relationship under the Civil Partnership Act 2004 formed by two persons of the same sex who both are aged 16 or over. The registration procedures are similar to those of marriage. For tax purposes, civil partners are treated in the same way as spouses in a marriage.

Class A shares. Shares that usually carry no voting rights.

Clean price. The price of a *Bond* excluding the *Interest accrual*. The underlying capital value of the bond. Bond prices are usually quoted on a clean basis. The actual price paid will be the clean price with an interest accrual adjustment. This total price is known as the *Dirty price*.

Clearing (or clearance). In securities and *Derivatives* trading, the practice post-trade and pre-settlement of defining settlement obligation and assigning responsibility for effecting *Settlement*.

Clearing member. An entity that is a member of a clearing house and thus has the ability to clear transactions. Contrast with a *Non-clearing member*, who cannot clear directly via the clearing house, and must therefore employ the services of a clearing member to clear trades on his behalf. See also *General clearing member* and *Individual clearing member*.

Clearstream. A *Clearing* and *Settlement* agency whose core business is to ensure that cash and securities are promptly and effectively delivered against each other in clearing and settling market transactions. Part of the Deutsche Börse group, Clearstream has two divisions - Clearstream Banking Luxembourg (the *International Central Securities Depository* or ICSD) and Clearstream Banking Frankfurt – the German domestic CSD. Clearstream offers settlement and *Custody* service to more than 2,500 customers in 94 global locations worldwide, covering over 150,000 domestic and internationally-traded bonds and equities. See also *Euroclear*.

Click. The computer-based trading platform operated by the *OM Exchange (OMX)* in Stockholm.

Client. A person to whom an authorised firm provides a service in the course of carrying on a *Regulated activity* or, in the case of *MiFID* or equivalent third country business, a person to whom a firm provides an *Ancillary service*. The term 'client' encompasses those from the smallest *Retail client* through to the largest investment firm. It includes, under the terminology of *MiFID*, *Eligible counterparties*, *Professional clients* and *Retail clients*.

Client money. The money of any currency that a firm holds in respect of any investment agreement with a client. The custody and client money rules for *MiFID business* are to be found in *CASS* 6 and 7. Client money, under MiFID rules, must be deposited with a *Central bank*, an *EEA* credit institution, a bank authorised in a third country, or a qualifying money market fund. The *FSA's* CASS 4 Client Money Rules (CMRs) apply to a firm that receives or holds money for or on behalf of a client in connection with its *Designated investment business*. The CMRs are not intended to cover regular deposit or savings accounts which are covered by separate banking codes. Key objectives of the CMRs are to seek to protect client money from the claims of creditors in the event of a firm's insolvency, and to prevent firms misusing client funds, e.g. to finance their businesses.

Clients' best interests rule. The *COBS* rule (COBS 2.1) requiring that firms must act honestly, fairly and professionally in accordance with the best interests of the client. This rule applies to designated investment business for a *Retail client* or, in relation to *MiFID* business, for any other client.

Close (out). A transaction that extinguishes commitments to the markets, i.e. a purchase if the initial transaction was a sale and *vice versa*. See *Closing purchase* and *Closing sale*.

Close period. See *Model Code for Directors' Dealings*.

Closing auction. A period of five minutes (plus possible extensions), starting at 16:30, in which limit and market orders may be input into the *SETS* system. No *Automatic matching* occurs until the end of the auction when the uncrossing algorithm is run. This will normally give the closing price for that security.

Closing order. An order type used where the order must be executed during the official closing period in the market concerned.

Closing purchase. A transaction in which a position is purchased to cancel a sold position already established. See *Offset*.

Closing sale. A transaction in which a position is sold to cancel a purchased position already established. See *Offset*.

Closing trade. See *Offset*.

CMA. See *Cash Memorandum Account*.

CME Group. The combined entity formed by the 2007 merger of the *Chicago Mercantile Exchange (CME)* and the *Chicago Board of Trade (CBOT)*. CME Group provides a wide range of benchmark futures and options products, covering all major asset classes. In early 2008, CME Group was discussing a deal to take over *New York Mercantile Exchange (NYMEX)*.

COBS. The abbreviation for the post-*MiFID* Conduct of Business Sourcebook, which is part of the *FSA Handbook*.

Code of Market Conduct. The Code providing guidance on what constitutes *Market abuse* and which *Safe harbours* are deemed not to be abusive.

Code of Practice for Approved Persons. A Code setting out conduct which the *FSA* believes would breach the *Statements of Principle for Approved Persons*. The Code is not conclusive: it is only evidential towards indicating that a Statement of Principle has been breached. Account will be taken of the context in which the course of conduct was undertaken.

Cold calling. Making unsolicited contact with a customer. Firms may only make cold calls ('unwritten *Financial promotions*') if the recipient has an established client relationship with the firm, such that the recipient envisages receiving them, or the call is about a generally marketed *Packaged product* (not based on a high volatility fund), or the call relates to controlled activities by an authorised person or exempt person, involving only readily realisable securities (not warrants). The person calling must do so at an appropriate time of day, identify himself and his firm, and makes his purpose clear, clarify if the client wants to continue or terminate the communication, and terminate it on request at any time and, if an appointment is arranged, gives a contact point to the client.

COLL. The FSA Sourcebook for certain *Collective investment schemes*. COLL contains rules that a regulated collective investment scheme (such as an authorised *Unit trust* or an *Open-Ended Investment Company*) must comply with in order to attain and maintain regulated status for the scheme. The rules include provisions on borrowing, investments the scheme can buy, pricing reports and accounts. In order to get regulated status for a scheme, the manager and trustee (who will usually be FSA-authorised firms) must apply to the *FSA* under s242 *FSMA 2000*.

Collateralised Debt Obligation (CDO). A type of asset-backed *Structured finance* product. CDOs are backed by a portfolio of fixed income securities, and are structured according to *Credit ratings*.

Collective investment scheme. A system for pooled investment in securities, by means of which investors' resources are combined together in a single investment vehicle. This is achieved through the medium of *Unit trusts, OEICs* or *Investment trusts*. The benefit to the small investor is the ability to spread his limited resources over a wider pool of investments giving the benefit of diversification, and to profit from the expertise of the fund manager running the scheme. Known in the USA as mutual funds. See also *Undertakings for Collective Investment in Transferable Securities* (UCITS) and *Open-Ended Investment Companies* (OEICs).

Combination. An *Options* trade involving both calls and puts on the same *Underlying asset* e.g. buy a call and buy a put option with the same *Strike price* for the same delivery month in the same underlying product (known as a *Long straddle*). Contrast with an option *Spread* trade, where the trade consists of either all calls or all puts.

Combined Code on Corporate Governance. A code on corporate governance published by the *UKLA* (United Kingdom Listing Authority) following the issue of the final report of the Hampel Committee. The Code is derived from the recommendations of the Hampel, Greenbury and Cadbury and Higgs reports concerning corporate governance. The UKLA requires companies to disclose in their annual reports both how they have applied the principles of good governance and whether they have complied with the provisions of the code of best practice.

Combined IDD. See *Initial Disclosure Document (IDD)*.

COMEX. New York Commodities Exchange, which is a division of the *New York Mercantile Exchange (NYMEX)*.

Command economy. A State-controlled economy in which production is centrally organised and decisions are typically taken by central planning committees.

Commercial bills (also known as trade bills). Promises to pay issued by companies (usually medium-sized) and usually guaranteed ('accepted') by a bank. They pay no interest and hence are issued at a discount to *Nominal value*. They have varying maturities. They may be eligible bills, indicating that the *Bank of England* is prepared to purchase them in the *Money markets*.

Commercial paper. Also known as CP or ECP (Euro Commercial Paper). Borrowing in the form of short-term paper issued by companies. Usually redeemable at *Par* value and paying no interest: hence it is generally issued at and trades at a discount.

Commodities. For investment purposes, essentially raw materials that can be bought and sold easily in large quantities on organised markets. See *Hard commodities* and *Soft commodities*.

Commodity Futures Trading Commission (CFTC). The US *Futures* regulator.

Commodity swap. An arrangement in which the counterparty offers a series of cash-settled futures contracts to the hedger. The hedger is offered a single fixed price, at which he will notionally buy or sell on an agreed date. Cash settlement is calculated on the difference between the fixed price and the price of an agreed index for a stated notional amount of the underlying asset. Commodity swaps enable users to immunise their price risk to a particular commodity for periods of up to ten years. Unlike *Interest rate swaps*, commodity swaps are predominantly hedging vehicles.

Common platform. The organisational and systems and controls requirements of *MiFID* and the *Capital Requirements Directive (CRD)* are implemented through a single set of high level rules. This is known as the 'common platform', since it applies to firms commonly, whichever of the Directives they are subject to. Firms subject to both MiFID and CRD include most banks and investment firms. Firms subject to MiFID only are those authorised to provide investment advice and/or receive and transmit orders without having permission to hold client money or securities. Firms subject to CRD only include banks that do not perform any investment services or other activities within the scope of MiFID.

Common stock. See *Ordinary shares*.

Commutation. Giving up part of the entitlements under a pension plan in return for a lump sum.

Company limited by guarantee. An incorporated body in which the liability of the shareholders on winding up is limited by the amount they undertook to contribute on incorporation. Usually these amounts are very small.

Comparability concept. The principle in accounting that it should be possible to make comparisons of the financial statements of different businesses, and it should be possible to make comparisons between the statements of the same enterprise for different periods. This concept of comparability should be ensured if information is measured and reported in similar ways in different businesses and in different periods.

Comparative advantage. The advantage in the production of a good that is enjoyed by one country over another when the good can be produced at a lower opportunity cost than in the other country.

Compensation Order. The power of the *FSA* to require a defendant to pay compensation.

Competent authority. The *UK Listing Authority* – the *FSA* – which has been designated as the competent authority under the *FSMA 2000* Part VI for the purpose of regulating companies that are seeking an *Official listing*.

Competent employees rule. A rule stating that firms must employ personnel with the skills, knowledge and expertise necessary for the discharge of the responsibilities allocated to them. This rule is now the main *FSA Handbook* requirement relating to the competence of employees. The rule is included in SYSC (3.1.6 and 5.1.1) and applies to all *Authorised firms* – non-MiFID firms as well as *MiFID* firms – including wholesale firms.

Competition Commission. The statutory body that is responsible for investigating mergers and takeovers in the UK to ensure that they do not lead to a substantial lessening of competition. The Competition Commission will investigate a merger at the instigation of the *Office of Fair Trading* and will make the final decision as to whether the merger should be cleared or blocked.

Complaints Commissioner. An independent investigator of complaints against the *FSA* arising from the discharge of its functions. The Commissioner is able to report publicly and recommend compensation payments.

Complements. Goods that are normally consumed in combination, for example cars and petrol. As the price of cars falls, the demand for cars will rise and, as a consequence, so will the demand for petrol.

Concert party. See *Acting in concert*.

Conclusive provision. The letter 'C' is used in the *FSA Handbook* to indicate that the provision is a conclusive provision. Such provisions are found in relation to the civil offence of *Market abuse*. Conclusive provisions (also referred to as *Safe harbours*) describe behaviour that does not amount to market abuse.

Conduct of Business rules. Detailed rules issued by the *Financial Services Authority* and included in its *Handbook* as the Conduct of Business Sourcebook (*COBS*) that govern a firm's relationship with its customers.

Confirmation. The document which outlines the details of a trade just undertaken and which must be sent out promptly to the customer.

Conflict of interest. *FSA*-authorised firms are required to identify conflicts of interest, to have an effective written conflicts of interest policy and to keep an up-to-date record of all past and present conflict situations.

CONNECT. See *LIFFE CONNECT®*.

Consistency concept. The principle that a firm must prepare its accounts on a consistent basis year on year, to facilitate comparisons. The same accounting methods should normally be applied from one period to the next. For example, there should not be repeated changes to the method of *Depreciation* of assets in the accounts. When changes are made, they should be explained and justified. As long as accounting methods are applied consistently, variation in measured results from period to period should reflect variations in performance and not accounting changes.

Consolidated Stock (or Consols). A name for several issues of UK Government bonds, the most common of which is 2.5% Consolidated Stock.

Consolidation of control. In the *City Code on Takeovers and Mergers*, a situation in which an investor or *Concert party* owns between 30% and 50% inclusive of the voting rights in

BPP))) LEARNING MEDIA

company and buys more shares. If this occurs, the investor will be required to make a mandatory offer for all the other shares in the company.

Consumer's hedge. An alternative term for a *Long hedge*.

Consumer Price Index (CPI). A harmonised measure used across the EU to measure the rate of change of prices, i.e. *Inflation*. The CPI is the measure targeted by the *Monetary Policy Committee* of the *Bank of England* in their monetary policy. See also *Retail Prices Index*.

Contango. In *Futures* markets, a situation in which the *Spot* or nearby prices (cash prices) are lower than longer-term prices (futures prices). The opposite of *Backwardation*. Sometimes such markets are said to be 'at a premium'.

Contingent liability transaction. A *Derivatives* transaction under which the customer may be required to pay money after the trade date, i.e. any type of margined trade.

Continuing obligations. The ongoing rules of the *UK Listing Authority*, detailed in the *Listing Rules*, which have to be followed by a listed company. An example is the requirement to disclose price-sensitive information via a *Regulatory Information Service*.

Continuous auction. See *Instant auction*.

Continuous Linked Settlement (CLS). CLS Bank is a private initiative supported by the largest foreign exchange banks to eliminate settlement risk and reduce the systemic liquidity risk in the foreign exchange *(FX)* market. CLS is a real-time system that enables simultaneous settlement globally, irrespective of time zones. CLS is an ongoing process of: submitting instructions – receiving payments of specified currencies from customers; funding – settling pairs of instructions that satisfy all criteria; and execution – making pay-outs in specified currencies. Settlement is final and irrevocable, or funds are returned same day.

Contract. The standard unit of trading for *Futures* and *Options* – sometimes also referred to as a 'lot'. Trades can only be effected in whole contracts.

Contract for Differences (CfD). A *Contract* whose price tracks the price of an *Underlying asset*, while the CfD holder does not take ownership of the asset. The underlying asset might be a company's shares, a *Bond*, a currency, a *Commodity* or an index. Investors can use CfDs to take a *Short position* – and thus gain from price declines, but they lose if the price rises. A CfD is within the *FSA's* definition of a *Derivative*.

Contract note. An alternative term for a *Confirmation*.

Contract size. The amount of the *Underlying asset* which one *Futures* contract represents, e.g. the contract size for a copper contract is 25 tonnes. This means that underlying one copper future is 25 tonnes of copper that the investor has the obligation to buy (long future) or sell (short future).

Contract specification. The legal document produced by an exchange that sets out the details of a *Futures* or *Options* contract, e.g. trading times, delivery procedures and quantities of underlying per one contract. The use of contract specifications leads to standardised products and thus maintains *Liquidity*.

Contracted out. A situation of having given up benefits under the *State Second Pension (S2P)* scheme in order to receive benefits under an *Occupational* or *Personal pension scheme* instead.

Control. (1) For legal purposes, usually owning in excess of 50% of the voting rights of a company or having the right to appoint directors on the company's board with a majority of voting rights. (2) For *City Code* purposes, owning 30% of a company gives effective control. If an investor obtains control of a company covered by the *City Code*, he is obliged to make a mandatory offer to buy out all the other shareholders. (3) For *Listing Rules* purposes, see *Controlling shareholder*.

Controlled function. For *FSA*-authorised firms, a list of specific roles (found in the *FSA Handbook*) which require the persons performing them to prove they are fit and proper and to become approved persons.

Controlling shareholder. For the purpose of the *Listing Rules*, an investor holding 30% or more of a listed company's shares. Such a shareholder will only be permitted for a listed company if it can be demonstrated that any conflicts of interest arising between the controlling shareholder and the interests of other shareholders will be suitably managed.

Conventional gilt. The term used to describe all *Gilts* except index-linked gilts.

Convergence. The process by which *Futures* prices and cash prices move together as delivery approaches. Convergence occurs on the final day of trading of the future, when there is no longer any *Cost of carry* included in its price. At this point the futures price equals the cash price.

Conversion. An example of an *Arbitrage* trade, where a *Future* is purchased and a synthetic future is sold by buying a put option and selling a call option with the same *Maturity* and *Strike price* on the same *Underlying asset*. Entered into when the relationship described as *Put/call parity* has broken down, and the future is relatively cheap to the synthetic. The opposite of a *Reversal*.

Convertible debt. Debt where the lender has the option to convert the debt into *Ordinary shares* in the company rather than receiving repayment in cash.

Convertible gilt. A UK Government bond *(Gilt)*, where the holder of the bond has the option to convert the bond into another issue of Government bonds rather than receive repayment in cash.

Core services. In the *MiFID* framework, the investment services and activities which fall under MiFID regulation that are not 'non-core' *Ancillary services*.

Corporate actions. A generic term referring to actions taken by a company with regard to its shareholders. This will include payment of *Dividends*, *Bonus* or *Rights issues* and voting at meetings.

Corporate bond. A *Bond* issued by a corporation.

Corporation tax. Taxation payable in the UK by companies, as opposed to individuals and trusts, who pay Income Tax and Capital Gains Tax. The rate of corporation tax varies depending on the 'size' of the company, as measured by taxable profits.

Correlation. A measure of how two variable factors move in relation to each other. correlation coefficient will have any value between +1 and -1. If the returns from two securities are perfectly positively correlated then they move up and down together in equal proportion. If the returns from two securities are perfectly negatively correlated then they move up and down in exact opposition and in proportion. If the returns from two securities are uncorrelated then they move independently of each other, i.e. if one goes up, the other may go up or down or not move at all.

Cost of carry. The costs incurred in buying an asset today and carrying it through to the delivery day of a *Future*. Such costs may include finance costs, insurance and storage, and will be reduced by the benefits of holding certain assets such as *Dividends* and *Coupons*.

Cost push inflation. *Inflation* resulting from an increase in the costs of production of goods and services.

Council of the European Union. Sometimes called the Council of Ministers, the Council shares powers to make laws with the *European Parliament* and also co-ordinates economic and foreign policy. With the *European Parliament*, it sets the EU budget. The Presidency of the European Council rotates every six months. Matters are agreed by voting, with some Member States having more votes than others.

Counterparty. The other party in a bilateral agreement, transaction or contract.

Counterparty risk. See *Credit risk*.

Country risk (or sovereign risk). Risk arising from the particular country in which or with which business is conducted.

Country risks: examples

- Market open to manipulation
- Rapid expansion of newly listed securities caused by the dash for growth
- Volatile trading activity
- Conflicting and ineffective (by mature market standards) regulatory environment   and structures
- Lack of and poor quality of information
- Physical share certificates
- Lack of automated settlement processes
- Fraud
- Low liquidity

Coupon. The rate of interest payable on a *Bond*. For example, a bond with a 10% coupon and a nominal value of £100 will pay gross annual interest of £10 in total, regardless of the price at which the bond is trading in the market.

Coupon stripping. Taking a *Coupon* paying *Bond* and selling on each of its coupons separately as *Zero coupon bonds*, known as *Strips*.

Coupon swap. An arrangement involving the exchange of a fixed interest rate (e.g. the coupon payment on a bond) for the floating rate, as measured by an index such as *LIBOR*. These are sometimes called fixed against floating or generic swaps.

Covenant. A stipulation in a loan agreement restricting the borrower's freedom of action while the loan is outstanding, so as to protect the interests of the lender.

Covered. A position is described as covered if the cash or asset to be delivered by the contractual obligation in the derivatives position is already held. For example, if you sell a copper future and thereby become obligated to deliver 25 tonnes of copper, you would be covered if you already held the copper. Not to be confused with *Margin*. Contrast with *Naked*.

Covered warrant. A *Warrant* on the shares of a company or on an index. Covered warrants are issued by a financial institution, where the institution has hedged its position in the underlying stock, usually by holding the securities in question. Both call warrants, giving the right to buy at a specified price within a specified time period, and put warrants, giving a right to sell at a specified price within a specified period, are available.

CP. See *Commercial paper*.

CPI. See *Consumer Price Index*.

Credit. The use or possession of goods or services without immediate payment. There are the following types: consumer credit, trade credit for companies, and bank credit which consists of loans and overdrafts to bank customers. As part of the *Money supply*, credit has great economic significance. A credit item is a liability, provision, or *Shareholders' funds* balance in a company *Balance sheet*, as well as an item of income or increasing profits in the *Income statement* (*profit and loss account*).

Credit crunch. A reduction in availability of loans and other types of credit from banks and the capital markets at prevailing *Interest rates*. A credit crunch hit the US and other economies during 2007/08, with tightened lending standards following a decline in the housing market.

Credit default swap (CDS) (or credit swap). A bilateral *Over-the-counter (OTC)* contract designed to trade separately the *Credit risk* of one or more third party entities. With a CDS, the protection seller agrees to make a payment to the protection buyer on the occurrence of a specified credit event in exchange for a fixed payment. The most common type of credit *Derivative*.

Credit institution. Credit institutions (banks and *Building societies*, in the UK) are regulated by the *Banking Consolidation Directive (BCD)* rather than *MiFID*. However, most MiFID provisions will apply to these institutions when they engage in activities within MiFID's scope.

Credit multiplier. The ability of banks to create *Credit*, and hence money, by maintaining their cash reserves at less than 100% of the value of their deposits.

Credit rating. An indicator for potential investors of the level of security that they expect from a particular *Bond* issuer. The three main agencies offering credit ratings are Moody's, Standard & Poor's and Fitch, whose rating systems are set out in the following Table.

Investment grade (Prime)			Non-investment grade (Non-prime or Junk)		
Standard & Poor's	Moody's	Fitch	Standard & Poor's	Moody's	Fitch
AAA	Aaa	AAA	BB+	Ba1	BB+
AA+	Aa1	AA+	BB	Ba2	BB
AA	Aa2	AA	BB−	Ba3	BB−
AA−	Aa3	AA−	B+	B1	B+
A+	A1	A+	B	B2	B
A	A2	A	B−	B3	B−
A−	A3	A−	CCC	Caa	CCC
BBB+	Baa1	BBB+	CC	Ca	
BBB	Baa2	BBB	C	C	
BBB−	Baa3	BBB−	D		

The explanations below are based on Standard & Poor's ratings.

AAA	**Debt rated AAA has the highest rating assigned by Standard & Poor's. Capacity to pay interest and repay principal is extremely strong.**
AA	**Debt rated AA has a very strong capacity to pay interest and repay principal and differs from the higher rated issues only in small degree.**
A	**Debt rated A has a strong capacity to pay interest and repay principal although it is somewhat more susceptible to the adverse effects of changes in circumstances and economic conditions than debt in higher rated categories.**
BBB	**Debt rated BBB is regarded as having an adequate capacity to pay interest and repay principal. Adverse economic conditions or changing circumstances are more likely to lead to a weakened capacity to pay interest and repay principal for debt in this category than in higher rated categories. BBB and above are investment grades.**
BB, B, CCC, CC, C	**Debt rated BB, B, CCC, CC and C is regarded, on balance, as predominantly speculative with respect to capacity to pay interest and repay principal in accordance with the terms of the obligation. While such debt will likely have some quality and protective characteristics, these are outweighed by large uncertainties or major risk exposures to adverse conditions.**
CI	**The rating CI is reserved for income bonds on which no interest is being paid.**
D	**Debt rated D is in default, and payment of interest and/or repayment of principal is in arrears.**

Credit risk (or counterparty risk). The risk that a counterparty will fail to complete a financial transaction according to the agreed terms, resulting in a loss.

Critical yield. When using the *Transfer Value Analysis System (TVAS)* for a pension transfer, the critical yield represents the investment return required for the pension scheme accepting the transfer to provide benefits equivalent to those which the *Occupational pension scheme* from which a transfer is to be made would provide at retirement.

Creditors. Those to whom money is owed. Liabilities of a company, representing amounts due to third parties. Creditors are analysed in the *Balance sheet* into current liabilities and non-current liabilities.

CREST. A *Recognised Clearing House (RCH)* enabling certificated and uncertificated settlement (see *Dematerialisation*) of UK and Irish equities, gilts and corporate loan stocks. CREST's benefits are more apparent as a paperless system facilitating faster settlement including T + 0. In 2000, CREST is also the primary settlement system for *Gilts*. CREST is now part of the Euroclear group.

CREST Courier and Sorting Service (CCSS). Part of *CREST* that deals with paperwork associated with settlement.

CREST Depository Interests (CDIs). Similarly to *American Depository Interests (ADRs)* in the USA, CREST Depository Interests (CDIs) offer a way of acquiring rights in foreign shares for UK investors. CDIs are offered on the London Stock Exchange International Retail Service. CDIs can be bought in *Sterling* and usually there is no *Stamp duty* to pay.

CREST member. A *CREST participant* holding dematerialised stock (see *Dematerialisation*) in stock accounts. A member is the legal owner of the securities and will appear in the company register. CREST members include *Market makers*, *Broker-dealers*, *Inter-dealer brokers*, *Stock borrowing and lending intermediaries*, institutional investors and *Custodians*. The term generally means that the participant is a CREST user.

CREST member accounts. A facility permitting a *CREST member* with an undesignated (house) account to segregate different holdings, such as client holdings, in designated accounts.

CREST participant. A person or organisation who has a formal relationship with CREST. This would include *Members*, payment banks, *Registrars* and *Her Majesty's Revenue and Customs (HMRC)*.

CREST sponsored member. Certain investors, such as private investors and institutions who are active traders, wanting to hold stock in CREST accounts but lacking the direct technical access to CREST, can rely on another member or user of CREST. A sponsored member will appear in the register as the legal owner.

CREST stock account. Within each *CREST member account,* there is a stock account reflecting each individual line of stock held.

CREST user. A person or organisation with technical access permitting electronic communications with *CREST*.

Criminal offence. The Criminal law aims to deter persons, including companies, from committing criminal acts and to punish those who do. A criminal offence is punishable either in the Magistrates' Court or the Crown Court. The maximum penalty in the Magistrates' Court is six months in prison and/or a £5,000 fine. The maximum penalty in the Crown Court depends on the relevant statute. The burden of proof is 'beyond all reasonable doubt', unlike the 'balance of probabilities' test for a *Civil offence*.

Criminal Justice Act 1993. Legislation dealing with *Insider dealing*.

Cross-currency swap. A swap involving an exchange of interest streams in different currencies, of which at least one is at a *Floating rate* of interest. Such swaps could include cross-currency *Coupon swaps*, in which a fixed rate is exchanged for a floating rate, or cross currency *Basis swaps*, in which two floating rates in different currencies are exchanged.

Cross rates. The effective exchange rate achieved for two currencies across another currency. For example, a cross rate for *Sterling* and Swiss francs, where the customer wishes to sell sterling and buy Swiss francs, could be calculated by firstly converting the sterling into US dollars and then converting the US dollars into Swiss francs. Cross rates can be used to identify potential *Arbitrage* opportunities and to obtain quotes for currencies not commonly quoted against each other, sometimes referred to as exotic currencies.

Crossing. The situation in which a firm has both the buy side and the sell side of an order. Rules exist on *Derivative* exchanges governing the crossing of trades. Also known as self trading.

CSCE. The Coffee, Sugar and Cocoa Exchange, New York.

CTD. See *Cheapest to deliver*.

Cum dividend/Cum interest (or cum coupon). The trading status of a bond or share such that the purchaser of the bond or share is entitled to receive the next *Dividend* or interest

BPP)))
LEARNING MEDIA

payment respectively. The alternative is *Ex-dividend/Ex-interest* (or ex-coupon), where the seller of the bond or share retains the right to receive the next dividend or interest payment.

Currency swap. A swap involving the exchange of two fixed interest streams in different currencies with an exchange of *Principal* at *Maturity*.

Current account. The part of the *Balance of payments* that is due to trade flows. It can be broken down into visibles, which are physical goods imported into and exported from the United Kingdom, and invisibles, which are services imported to or exported from the UK, such as advertising, insurance and training.

Current assets. Assets that are not *Fixed* (or *'Non-current'*) *assets*. Current assets include cash plus assets that have usually been acquired with the intention of converting them into cash, such as *Inventories* (stocks), *Receivables* (debtors), short-term investments, cash and bank balances.

Current ratio. An accounting ratio usually defined as *Current assets* divided by *Creditors* falling due within one year. The ratio is designed to assess the solvency of a company in the short term. If the current ratio exceeds one, then the value of current assets is greater than the value of the short-term creditors, indicating that the company is able to pay its short-term debts as they fall due. Note that this interpretation is fairly simplistic.

CUSIP. An acronym used to refer to the nine-character alphanumeric security identifiers for all North American securities distributed by the Committee on Uniform Security Identification Procedures (CUSIP) to facilitate *Clearing* and *Settlement* of trades. In the 1980s there were moves to expand the CUSIP system to cover international securities. The resulting *CINS* (CUSIP International Numbering System) has however been little used as the truly international *ISIN* (International Securities Identifying Number) system has been widely adopted.

Custodian. The provider of a specialist service in the safe keeping of assets on behalf of other financial institutions and customers. A custodian specialises in looking after both physical and electronic/dematerialised stock and performs all the necessary *Reconciliations*. Today, the custody market is dominated by a few global players, primarily because the costs needed to compete require economies of scale to generate profitability. A domestic custodian operates in one local country, while a global custodian exists in all countries around the world. The global custodians offer additional services such as performance reporting, collecting income from corporate actions, record-keeping, cash management and stock lending. A global custodian might use a network of local sub-custodians.

Custody. The safekeeping (and often settlement) of investments that is a category of *Regulated activity* under *FSMA 2000*.

Custody assets. Designated investments and any other assets the firm holds in the same portfolio. See also *Safe custody investments*.

Customer. For most regulatory purposes, a *Client* who is not an *Eligible counterparty (ECP)*. Customers therefore include both *Professional clients* and *Retail clients*.

Customs union. An agreement among a group of two or more countries to remove customs restrictions among those countries and to impose a common external tariff on imports from outside the group. See also *Free trade area*.

Daily Official List. A *London Stock Exchange* publication giving details of share trading in the previous day, sometimes referred to as SEDOL (Stock Exchange Daily Official List).

Dark green fund. A *Fund* which applies an *SRI* or ethical investment approach, seeking high levels of screening and corporate social performance, compared with the lower levels of screening used by *Light green funds*.

Dark liquidity pools. A term referring to off-exchange trading. There are more than forty 'dark pool' trading platforms operating in the USA. They had originally developed to enable institutions to offload large blocks of stock without causing adverse price movements. Advances in technology and the *MiFID* rule changes, which are designed to promote competition, are factors encouraging the growth of off-exchange trading platforms in Europe.

DAX. The major German share price index, comprising 30 shares.

Dealing. Entering into transactions in investments either for customers or for the firm's own account.

Debenture. (1) A *Bond* issued with *Security* [UK]. (2) An unsecured *Bond* [US].

Debit. In accounting, a debit item is an asset balance in the *Balance sheet*, and an expense item, decreasing profits, in the *Income statement* (profit and loss account).

Debt/equity ratio. See *Gearing ratio*.

Debt Management Office. An Executive Agency of *HM Treasury* responsible for the issuance of *Gilts* and *Treasury bills*.

Debtors. See *Receivables*.

Declaration day. On the *LME*, the *Expiry* day of an *Option* contract.

Deep discount bond. A bond issued at a discount to *Par* value and redeemed at par or a premium to par. Such bonds may either pay a low *Coupon* over their lives (low coupon bonds) or no coupon at all (*Zero coupon bonds*). The difference between the issue price and the redemption price is effectively interest on the amount borrowed.

Default. Failure by a party to fulfil its obligations on debt repayments, or on a *Future* or *Option* contract when they fall due, including (for futures and options) failure to meet a *Margin* call, or to make or take delivery.

Defined benefit pension scheme. A scheme offering a pension based on the employee's salary and number of years' service with the company – alternatively known as a *Final salary pension scheme*.

Defined contribution pension scheme. A scheme offering a pension based on the eventual value of the invested contributions paid on behalf of the employee – also known as a *Money purchase pension scheme*.

Delivery. The settlement of a *Futures* or *Options* contract via the delivery of a physical asset or cash.

Delivery by value. The system by which *CREST* settles *Repos*.

Delivery versus Payment. *Settlement* arrangements that are simultaneous, thus ensuring that neither the buyer nor the seller is at risk from default, i.e. not having the cash or the securities. *CREST* provides such a structure. Alternatively referred to as *Cash Against Documents (CAD)*.

Delta. Drawn from the theory of *Options* pricing model *(*see *Black-Scholes model)*, the delta of an option shows the rate of change in an option premium with respect to a change in price of the underlying asset or security. For example, the premium on an option with a delta of 0.5 will move by 0.5p for every 1p move in the price of the underlying. Delta can also be defined as either (1) the probability that the option will expire in-the-money; or (2) the theoretical number of futures contracts of which the holder is either long (with a *Call option*) or short (*Put option*). The rate of change of delta is known as *Gamma*.

Delta hedged (or delta neutral). The situation where the net *Delta* of a portfolio of *Options and Futures* is zero, meaning that there is no exposure to directional movements in the underlying. However, that this does not mean that there is no risk attached to such a position. *Option* deltas change for a variety of reasons, and so the portfolio must be constantly readjusted in order to maintain a delta neutral position.

Demand. The quantity that potential purchasers will buy, or attempt to buy, at a given price.

Demand pull inflation. *Inflation* resulting from a persistent excess of aggregate demand over aggregate supply.

Dematerialisation. The holding of stock in electronic accounts within *CREST*, i.e. in uncertificated form, instead of being held as paper certificates, i.e. in certificated form.

Department for Business, Enterprise and Regulatory Reform (BERR). The UK Government department responsible *inter alia* for regulating the corporate sector.

Deposit set. A collection of documents required for a stock deposit to be made at *CREST*; a transfer form and the certificate or certified transfer form. See *Stock deposit* and *Certification*.

Depository. A clearing house or settlement agency whose primary role is to facilitate *Settlement*. Settlement delays are often caused by the time it takes for securities to be moved between counterparties. The settlement agency might therefore reduce these delays by holding the securities on behalf of customers. These securities will be held in the vault of the depository.

Depository receipts. See *American Depository Receipts (ADRs)*, *Global Depository Receipts (GDRs)*, *International Depository Receipts (IDRs)* and *Crest Depository Interests (CDIs)*.

Depreciation. Amounts charged to the *Income statement* (profit and loss account) to reflect the wearing out of a *Non-current asset* (fixed asset) over its estimated useful economic life. For example, if a company buys a car for £10,000 with an expected useful life of four years, it will charge the £10,000 cost to profit and loss account over a four-year period. The simplest way to do this is to charge £2,500 expense per year (straight-line depreciation). Since the benefit of the car is received over a four-year period, the cost of acquiring the car is charged against profits over a four-year period. Depreciation complies with the *Accruals concept*.

Derivatives. A term used to encompass products such as *Futures*, *Options* and *Swaps* which derive their value from the movement in price of an *Underlying asset*. *Derivatives* can be used to *Hedge* or to speculate, and risks can be high. The *FSA* defines a derivative as a *Contract for differences*, a future or an option.

Designated client account. A *Client money* bank account the monies in which may not be pooled with other 'general' client accounts.

Designated investment business. Activities defined by the *FSA* that relate generally to investments, such as stockbroking and fund management. It therefore does not include the other areas regulated by the FSA, such as general insurance and banking.

Designated Investment Exchange (DIE). An overseas exchange deemed by the FSA to provide an appropriate level of investor protection. Examples of DIEs include the Tokyo Stock Exchange and the New York Stock Exchange.

Designated Professional Body (DPB). DPBs are the professional bodies who govern the members of certain professions such as lawyers, accountants and actuaries. Although these professionals may sometimes be giving investment advice, as long as such activities do not constitute a major proportion of their business, i.e. are only incidental, they are exempt from the requirement to seek authorisation under *FSMA 2000*. However, they will still be governed by their professional bodies

Detective controls. Controls in an enterprise which detect errors once they have occurred. *Detective controls* are less ideal than *Preventive controls* but can still be effective in reducing risk. Internal detection controls detect errors before a potential loss is realised in the outside world. For example, checking the legal terms of a contract before it is signed is a control that may detect errors in the terms and conditions of the contract. External detection controls are those that detect errors and losses once they have been realised, such as post-settlement statement-to-ledger reconciliations.

Diagonal spread. An *Option spread* where one option is purchased and a different option is sold. The sold option has a different *Strike price* and *Expiry date* from the one purchased. The spread will be constructed with either all calls or all puts on the same *Underlying asset*.

DIE. See *Designated Investment Exchange*.

Diff swap. A diff(erential) or quanto swap is a special type of cross-currency *Basis swap*, which does not involve any exchange of principal whatsoever. Both streams of interest payments through a diff are calculated with reference to the same notional principal amount of the same currency. For example, a $/€ diff swap would typically involve an exchange of six-month LIBOR € for a six-month US LIBOR. Both *Interest rate* streams would be paid in euros.

Difference account. A document that sets out the profit/loss arising from the closing of a *Futures* position.

Dilution. The process whereby, as more shares are issued by a company, the interests of existing shareholders are diminished. *Earnings per share* of the company may be reduced as a result of the increased number of shares. A more specific meaning is used in the context of *Fully diluted earnings per share*.

Diminishing returns. The 'law' of diminishing returns states that, if one or more factors of production are fixed but the input of another is increased, then the extra output generated by each extra unit of input will eventually begin to fall.

Direct offer financial promotion. An advertisement (*Financial promotion*) providing a form or specifying a means of response, the completion of which, or response to which, creates an investment agreement.

Direct quote. In the *Forex (FX)* markets, an *Exchange rate* expressed in one currency – generally, the domestic currency – per unit of another currency. The opposite of an *Indirect quote*.

Directors' report. A report by a company's directors summarising the company's performance over the year, its future prospects and with certain other required disclosures. A legally required part of the company's *Annual report and accounts*.

Dirty price. The total price payable on the purchase of a *Bond*, given by the *Clean price* with an *Interest accrual* adjustment.

Disallowed expenditure. Expenses charged by a company in arriving at its accounting profit before tax which are not allowable as a deduction when calculating its taxable profits on which its *Corporation tax* charge is based. Examples include *Depreciation* (which is replaced by *Capital allowances* for tax purposes) and certain entertainment expenditure.

Discount. (1) When a bond is trading at a discount to *Par*, this indicates that its price is lower than its *Nominal value*. (2) When a currency is at a discount in the forward *FX* markets, this indicates that it is weakening in the forward market relative to the spot market. As a result the forward discount is added to the spot rate quote.

Discretionary management. An investment arrangement where the firm decides when and what investments to invest in within restrictions / objectives outlined by the customer. The delegation of decision making to the firm carries significant risks for the customer and consequently, such customers have additional regulatory protection.

Dispersion. The measure of variability or spread of values around a central point of location.

Distance contract. A *Contract* which is concluded under an 'organised distance sales service-provision scheme' directly or through an intermediary with exclusive use of one more means of distance communication.

Distance Marketing Directive (DMD). A European Directive which came into force in 2004 and which extended the requirement to provide cancellation rights and certain documentation to *Retail customers* dealt with at a distance. Under the *FSA's* original rules, cancellation rights were only generally provided where private customers purchased packaged products such as life policies. Under the DMD, cancellation rights and documentation apply to a wider range of cases, including securities broking services provided at a distance.

Diversification. The process of holding a range of investments in order to diversify risk, so that if one investment performs badly, this may be compensated by better returns from the remainder of the portfolio.

Dividend cover. An accounting ratio defined as net earnings per *Ordinary (equity) share* divided by net dividend per ordinary share. The purpose of the ratio is to identify how much of a company's profits are being distributed to shareholders and how much is being retained to finance future expansion of the business. Generally, a company with a low dividend cover is paying out most of its earnings as dividends and is unlikely to achieve high growth in the future, compared to a company with high dividend cover.

Dividend yield. An accounting ratio, defined as the dividend per share divided by the share price. Broadly speaking, the lower the dividend yield, the higher the company's share price and the more highly rated the company.

Dividends. Amounts paid to shareholders, typically annually or semi-annually in the case of UK companies, representing a return on their investment in the company. *Preference shares* receive a fixed dividend while for *Ordinary (Equity) shares* the level of dividend depends on profitability.

DJIA. See *Dow Jones Industrial Average*.

DMO. See *Debt Management Office*.

Domicile. A legal term indicating the country to whose legal system an individual is attached. Most people acquire their domicile at birth, being the domicile of their father. This is referred to as the domicile of origin.

Double-dated stocks. *Bonds* where the issuer has the option to redeem the stock on or between two specified dates.

Double entry bookkeeping. The method on which accounting is based, which derives from the *Accounting equation* and the fundamental principle that each transaction has two sides or effects. The notation of the double entry method is based on the principle that for each transaction there are two entries, a 'debit' entry and a 'credit' entry. A debit entry represents an increase in an asset or a decrease in a liability. A credit entry represents an increase in a liability or *Shareholders' funds* or a decrease in an asset. See also *Dual aspect concept*.

Double taxation agreements (or tax treaties). Bilateral agreements between nations dealing with the situation of individuals or businesses who are resident in one country and have income or gains in another. The agreements generally seek to address and avoid the inequitable possibility that a taxpayer might be liable to pay tax on the same income or gains in both jurisdictions.

Dow Jones Industrial Average (DJIA, or 'The Dow'). A widely followed index of the prices of leading US shares and globally the best known of all share price indices. The Dow now contains 30 stocks, chosen by Dow Jones and the *Wall Street Journal*, which are designed to represent a balanced selection of *Blue chips*. In recent years, the constituents have gradually been altered, to reflect the shift in the US economy away from traditional manufacturing towards computers and service industries. The Dow is a price-weighted index, so a move in the share price of a company with relatively modest *Market capitalisation* can have as great an influence on the day's price movements as a comparable move in the price of a large one. This effect is partially reduced by the selection of very large companies, and by the tendency for US companies to manage the nominal value of their shares to ensure market prices that fall into a roughly comparable range, between $30 and $100. The original base number for the Dow was 100 and the index is calculated in real time.

Dual aspect concept. The fundamental principle in accounting that each transaction has two sides or effects. A transaction is anything the company does which affects its financial position such as buying an asset, paying its employees, taking out a loan or making a sale. See also *Double entry bookkeeping*.

Dual capacity. The ability of a firm to act either as *Principal* with the customers when trading or to act as *Agent* on behalf of their customers. See also *Agent, Principal* and *Broker-dealer*.

Durable medium. For the purpose of communications by *FSA*-authorised firms, 'durable medium' means either paper, or an instrument (e.g. an email message) which enables the recipient to store information addressed personally to him in a way accessible for future reference for a period of time adequate for the purposes of the information and which allows the unchanged reproduction of the information stored. This will include the recipient's computer hard drive or other storage devices on which the electronic mail is stored, but no Internet websites unless they fulfil the criteria in this definition. Where a rule requires a notice to be delivered in writing, a firm may comply using electronic media. The *COBS* rules often specify that communication must be in a durable medium.

Duration. A measure of the volatility of a *Bond* or the sensitivity of the bond's price to changes in *Interest rates*. Defined as the weighted average of the number of years in the bond's life, the weighting factor being the present value of the cash flows in the year discounted at the *Internal rate of return* of the bond's cash flows.

DvP. See *Delivery versus payment*.

Earnings. Often used generally to mean 'profits'. Earnings does, however, have a very specific definition in the context of *Earnings per share*, when it is defined as profit after tax, *Minority interests*, *Extraordinary items* and *Preference dividends*. The objective of the calculation is to arrive at an earnings figure that is attributable to *Ordinary (equity) shareholders*. As a result, all charges that rank prior to the Ordinary shareholders are deducted in the calculation.

Earnings per share (EPS). A measure of a company's profitability from the point of view of *Ordinary shareholders*. See *Earnings*. EPS is defined as earnings attributable to equity shareholders divided by the number of equity shares in issue over the year. See also *Fully diluted earnings per share*.

Earnings yield. An accounting ratio defined as net *Earnings per share* divided by the share price. Broadly speaking, the lower the earnings yield, the higher the company's share price and the more highly rated the company.

Economies of scale. Factors which cause *Average cost* to decline in the long run as output increases.

ECP. See *Commercial paper*.

EDC. See *Electronic data capture*.

EDSP. See *Exchange Delivery Settlement Price*.

EDX London. A business providing *Derivatives* market services specifically tailored for equity market participants and developed by the *LSE* and OM AB. EDX London attempts to combine the strength of *London Stock Exchange's* global equity market offering and expertise with OM's flexible technology and experience in equity derivatives.

EEA. See *European Economic Area*.

EFFAS. See *European Federation of Financial Analysts' Societies*.

Efficient Markets Hypothesis (EMH). A theory that states broadly that, at any time, share prices are fairly valued on the basis of all existing information.

EFP. See *Exchange For Physical*.

EGM. See *Extraordinary General Meeting*.

EIRIS. See *Ethical Investment Research Service*.

EIS. See *Enterprise Investment Scheme*.

Elasticity. The concept that economists use to explain the degree of sensitivity demand exhibits in respect of various factors. The factors include: the price of the good, in the case of the price elasticity of demand (PED); incomes, in the case of income elasticity of demand (YED); and the price of other goods, in the case of cross elasticity of demand (XED).

Elective eligible counterparty. An *Eligible counterparty (ECP)* who has chosen that status and meets certain conditions, as follows. A firm may treat an undertaking as an elective eligible counterparty if the client is a *per se Professional client* (unless it is such by virtue of being an institutional investor); or is an elective professional client and requests the categorisation, but only in respect of the transactions and services for which it counts as a professional client; and, in the case of *MiFID* or equivalent third country business, provides 'express confirmation' of their agreement (which may be for a specific transaction or may be general) to be treated as an eligible counterparty. If the prospective counterparty is established in another *EEA* State, for *MiFID* business the firm should defer to the status determined by the law of that other State.

Elective professional client. See *Professional client*.

Electronic commerce activity (ECA). The Electronic Commerce Directive applies only to *ECA*, which is defined as the provision of *Information society services* from a place of business in the *EEA* which would require authorisation (i.e. be a *Regulated activity*) if it were provided by non-electronic means. Where ECA is being provided, the provider need not apply for authorisation in the host State via a full application, *Passporting* or *Treaty rights*. Firms doing ECA must comply only with their home State rules and minimum information requirements in the host State. (This concept of complying primarily with home State rules has been expanded to include most non-electronic cross-border business with the implementation of *MiFID*.)

Electronic data capture (EDC). The input into *CREST* of the details of a *Stock deposit*.

Eligible bills. Bills that the *Bank of England* is prepared to purchase in the *Money markets*.

Eligible complainant. A person eligible to have a complaint considered under the *Financial Ombudsman Service*. Eligible complainants comprise: private individuals, businesses with a group annual turnover of less than £1m, charities with an annual income of less than £1m or trusts with net asset value of less than £1m (other than those who are properly classified as *Professional clients* or *Eligible counterparties*) who are customers or potential customers of the firm.

Eligible counterparty (ECP). A *Client* who is either automatically treated as a *Per se Eligible counterparty* or is an *Elective eligible counterparty* and is subject to only 'light touch' regulation. Firms must allow *Professional clients* and eligible counterparties to re-categorise in order to get more regulatory protection. A *Per se Eligible counterparty* may be re-categorised as a *Professional client* or a *Retail client*.

Eligible counterparty business. Activities comprising: dealing on own account; execution of orders on behalf of *Eligible counterparty (ECP)* clients; reception and transmission of such orders; and related *Ancillary services*.

EMH. See *Efficient Markets Hypothesis*.

Emissions trading. See *Carbon trading*.

Endowment policy. A form of insurance-based policy that combines life insurance and savings. These policies are often associated with *Mortgages*: the savings element is designed to pay off the capital borrowed at the end of the term of the policy, and the *Life insurance* will repay the mortgage should the policyholder die before the end of that term.

Enduring Power of Attorney. See *Power of Attorney*.

Enhanced protection electing for enhanced protection allows an individual to avoid the Lifetime Allowance tax charge on pension benefits accrued by *'A-Day'* (i.e. by 5 April 2006), on the basis that he pays no further contributions and accrues no further benefit under registered pension schemes.

Enhanced scrip dividend. A *Scrip dividend* where the value of the shares distributed exceeds the value of the cash dividend foregone.

Enterprise Investment Scheme (EIS). A tax-subsidised arrangement to encourage investment in small risky companies. Where a company qualifies for the scheme, any investment in equity shares in the company qualifies for income tax relief at a rate of 20%, up to a maximum investment in the fiscal year in question. If the investor holds the shares for three years, any capital gain that he makes on disposing of the shares is free of tax. Any capital loss suffered on the shares is eligible as a deduction from other taxable capital gains. Although the tax reliefs are generous, there are a number of restrictions to prevent the scheme being used merely as a means of artificial tax avoidance.

Entity concept. The concept that a business or enterprise is treated, in accounting, as distinct and separate from its owners. It is necessary to separately record the assets and liabilities of the business, as well as its income and expenses, and to distinguish these from personal transactions of the owner.

EPS. See *Earnings per share*.

Equilibrium. The combination of the one level price and one level of output at which the amount producers are willing to supply and the amount consumers demand are equal.

Equities. See *Ordinary shares*.

Equity. See *Shareholders' funds* and *Ordinary shares*.

Equity swap. An arrangement in which the buyer pays the return on a money market deposit (e.g. LIBOR) and in exchange receives the total return on an equity investment (capital gains plus *Dividends*). The two payments are usually netted and are generally exchanged between two and four times annually. As with *Interest rate swaps*, no exchange of *Principal* is involved.

Escrow account. In takeover situations, this is a *CREST* facility that permits dematerialised stock to be transferred on behalf of accepting shareholders into this special account. The stock remains in the name of the holder, but under the control of the receiving agent (Escrow).

ETF. See *Exchange Traded Fund*.

Ethical Investment Research Service (EIRIS). An independent UK charity that researches ethical aspects of companies on behalf of other charities and fund managers.

EUREX. A European *Derivatives* exchange formed in 1998 by the merger of the Deutsche Terminbörse and the Swiss Options and Financial Futures Exchange. The world's largest derivatives exchange, with open interest on Eurex consistently exceeding 100 million contracts. A fully electronic exchange, Eurex allows market participants decentralised and standardised access to its markets on a global scale. Its listed contracts are financial futures and options together with a range of equity options and index *Futures* and *Options*. Trading on the fully computerised Eurex platform transcends borders and offers members technical access from any location, thereby creating a global liquidity network. To facilitate access to Eurex outside of Switzerland and Germany, access points have been installed in Amsterdam, Chicago, New York, Helsinki, London, Madrid, Paris, Hong Kong, Sydney and Tokyo. Over 50% of all Eurex trades emanates from London.

Euro commercial paper (ECP). See *Commercial paper*.

Euro zone. The group of EU Member States that have adopted the euro as their currency. The European Central Bank is responsible for monetary policy within the zone.

Euro zone countries

- Austria
- Belgium
- Cyprus
- Finland
- France
- Germany
- Greece
- Republic of Ireland
- Italy
- Luxembourg
- Malta
- Netherlands
- Portugal
- Slovenia
- Spain

(Slovakia is expected to join in 2009)

Eurobond. A bond issued outside of the country in whose currency it is denominated. For example, a Eurobond denominated in US dollars is issued outside of the US. (The term has no relation to the *Euro zone*.)

Euroclear. Euroclear and *Clearstream* are *Clearing* and *Settlement* agencies that both settle transactions in a large number of securities including all kinds of *Eurobonds*, domestic and foreign bonds, US Treasury and Agency bonds, short-term instruments (euro notes, *CDs*, *Bank bills* etc) and international and domestic equities and American/*Global Depositary Receipts*. Settlement is on a T+3 (third business day after trade) basis. *Clearstream* and Euroclear operate an electronic *Bridge* between each other. Within Euroclear and *Clearstream*, the stocks are physically immobilised within secure vaults, in comparison to *CREST* where the shares are held electronically. On *Settlement date* there is a book entry transfer to move stock from one account to another.

Euronext. A European securities and derivatives exchange formed through the merger of the Paris, Amsterdam and Brussels Stock Exchanges and MATIF. See *NYSE Euronext*.

Euronext.liffe. See *LIFFE*.

European Economic Area (EEA). Economic grouping incorporating all *European Union (EU)* States plus Iceland, Liechtenstein and Norway. The *Markets in Financial Instruments Directive (MiFID)* and *Passporting* apply across the EEA.

European Federation of Financial Analysts' Societies (EFFAS). A professional association for nationally-based investment professionals associations in Europe. The umbrella organisation comprises 24 member organisations, representing more than 14,000 investment professionals. EFFAS maintains its Head Office in Frankfurt am Main.

European Parliament. A body directly elected by the citizens of *European Union* Member States and meeting at least monthly. It shares powers to make laws with the *Council of the European Union*. supervises the *European Commission* and, with the *Council of the European Union*, sets the EU budget.

European Quoting Service (EQS). A *LSE* service enabling clients to meet their pre-trade pan-European transparency obligations. EQS is a *Quote-driven market* making and trade reporting platform that supports all EU liquid securities, excluding those traded on the *SETS, SETSqx, EUROSETS* and *ITBB* services. Initially, no electronic execution will be supported and *market makers* will enter non-electronically executable quotes during the *Mandatory Quote Period* (MQP). There will be no minimum number of *market makers* required per security.

European Savings Directive. A Directive requiring European States to exchange information automatically on the financial affairs of residents of other European States, or to levy a *Withholding tax*. The Directive affects EU residents who hold investments offshore within the EU or in Switzerland.

European-style option. An *Option* where the holder has the right to *Exercise* the option only on its *Expiry* date. Contrast with an *American-style option*, where the holder can *Exercise* up to and including the expiry date.

European Union (EU). Political and economic grouping of European Member States, numbering 27 by 2008.

European Union States (as of January 2008):

- Austria
- Belgium
- Bulgaria
- Cyprus
- Czech Republic
- Denmark
- Estonia
- Finland
- France
- Germany
- Greece
- Hungary
- Republic of Ireland
- Italy
- Latvia
- Lithuania
- Luxembourg
- Malta
- Netherlands
- Poland
- Portugal
- Romania
- Slovakia
- Slovenia
- Spain
- Sweden
- United Kingdom

European Economic Area comprises the EU *plus:*

- Iceland
- Liechtenstein
- Norway

EUROSETS™. The *London Stock Exchange's* Dutch Trading Service, which went live in 2004 – a first step in the *LSE's* drive to open up competition across the European markets. The Dutch Trading Service enables Exchange members to trade in the most liquid Dutch securities that form the AEX and AMX indices via the *SETS* Order Book. In October 2007, EUROSETS was enhanced to allow firms to be able to register as *Market makers* in any EUROSETS security.

Evidential provision. Provisions in the *FSA Handbook* that are linked to rules and set out circumstances in which the FSA will assume that the rule has been followed or breached. In the *Handbook*, the 'E' symbol indicates an evidential provision. Evidential provisions are rules that are not binding in their own right but rather derive their authority from linking to another rule. If a firm complies with an evidential provision, this will tend to establish compliance with the linked rule. If a firm breaches an evidential provision, this will tend to establish that a breach of the linked rule has occurred. In legal terms, evidential provisions provide a rebuttable presumption of compliance or non-compliance with the linked rule.

Ex-dividend/Ex-interest (or ex-coupon). The trading status of a bond or share such that the seller of the bond or share retains the right to receive the next dividend or interest payment respectively. The alternative is *Cum dividend* or *Cum interest*, in which case the purchaser has the right to receive the next dividend or interest payment.

Exceptional item. In a company's *Income statement*, an item which is material, derived from events or transactions within a company's ordinary activities and which needs to be disclosed separately to ensure that the company's accounts give a true and fair view. Compare with *Extraordinary item*.

Exchange Delivery Settlement Price (EDSP). The price at which *Futures* contracts are settled upon delivery. The EDSP is determined by the exchange, and is often an average of traded prices over a set period.

Exchange for Physical (EFP). In relation to *Futures*, the exchange between two customers of a physical and futures position, which is agreed directly between the two parties outside of the exchange on which the futures are dealt. EFPs are reported to the exchange, and documentary evidence of a physical transfer of goods may be required by the exchange. Also known as *Against actuals*.

Exchange rate. The ratio (price) at which two currencies are traded, i.e. the price of one currency in terms of another.

Exchange Traded Fund (ETF). A *Fund* which tracks an index, or a universe of securities with a particular pre-determined characteristic, with fund prices quoted in real-time during normal trading hours. Barclays Global Investors is a major issuer, using the trade mark iShares®.

Execution only. The relationship between a firm and client under which the client merely instructs the firm to buy or sell. No advice is provided by the firm and consequently, the suitability rules in *COBS* do not apply.

Execution policy. See *Order execution policy*.

Exercise. The process by which an *Option* holder takes up his right to buy (call) or sell (put) the *Underlying asset* for the option contract.

Exercise notice. The document sent by the holder of an *Option* contract to indicate they wish to *Exercise* their rights under the option.

Exercise price. The price at which an *Option* holder has the right to buy (call) or sell (put) the asset underlying the option contract. The contract specification will set out the exercise price intervals, e.g. 10p intervals. Also known as the *Strike price*.

Exercise style. Defines the date(s) that an *Option* holder has the right to *Exercise* his option. See *American-style option* and *European-style option*.

Expert private customer. See *Professional client*.

Expiry (date). The date after which an *Option* can no longer be either exercised or traded. This date will be specified in the contract specification.

External audit. An examination of the financial statements of an enterprise, performed by an external registered auditor. The scope and the methodology is in accordance with Companies Acts and auditing standards. The objective is to report to the members (shareholders) on whether the *Financial statements* give a 'true and fair' view and are in accordance with applicable *Accounting standards*.

Externalities. Effects of a transaction which extend beyond the parties to the transaction. The differences between the private and the social costs or benefits arising from an activity are externalities.

ExtraMARK. The part of the *London Stock Exchange* that trades *Exchange Traded Funds (ETFs)*.

Extraordinary General Meeting (EGM). An *ad hoc* shareholders' meetings held by a company for a specific purpose, such as to approve a major transaction. Fourteen calendar days' notice must be given of such a meeting, if only ordinary resolutions are to be discussed. If a special resolution is to be discussed, 21 calendar days' notice is normally required. The notice period may only be shortened if at least 95% of shareholders agree.

Extraordinary item. In a company's *Income statement*, an item that is material and possesses a high degree of abnormality, is not expected to recur and is derived from events or transactions outside of the ordinary activities of a company. Because the scope of ordinary activities is extremely wide, it is extremely unlikely that a company will show an extraordinary item in its *Financial statements* in any one year. Compare with *Exceptional item*.

F

Fair, clear and not misleading rule. The *FSA* rule which states that a firm must ensure that a communication or financial promotion is fair, clear and not misleading, as is appropriate and proportionate considering the means of communication and the information to be conveyed. The rule applies to communications in relation to *Designated investment business*, except communications directed at *Professional clients* or *Eligible counterparties* (i.e., 'non-retail' communications), certain excluded communications, and third party *Prospectuses*.

Fair value. In *Derivatives* terminology, the theoretical price at which a *Futures* or *Options* contract should trade.

Fast market. A situation where markets are hectic and turbulent such that prices are rapidly changing. As a result, prices quoted on electronic trading systems may not be up-to-date. In the UK, *SEAQ* prices become indicative rather than firm during a fast market as a result.

Federal Reserve Banks. The Central Banking system of the US, made up of a number of regional Federal Reserve Banks that regulate banking activities.

Fedwire. A *Real Time Gross Settlement (RTGS)* funds transfer system operated by the *Federal Reserve Banks*.

Fill. The execution of an order on the *Derivatives* market.

Final salary pension scheme. See *Defined benefits pension scheme*.

Financial Action Task Force (FATF). An inter-governmental body set up in 1989 and comprising members from around 30 countries worldwide, with headquarters in Paris. The FATF sets out international standards in respect of *Anti-money laundering*, terrorist financing and anti-fraud policies and procedures. This includes publishing recommendations for countries to implement laws, typologies of money laundering and other financial crime. The FATF also reviews countries' compliance with its recommendations and lists non co-operative countries, which financial institutions must take care when dealing with.

Financial gearing. For a company, financial *Gearing* is measured either by its *Gearing ratio* or by its *Interest Cover*.

Financial intermediary. A party bringing together providers and users of finance, either as a *Broker* facilitating a transaction between two other parties, or in their own right, as *Principal*.

Financial intermediation. The function fulfilled by *Financial intermediaries* (e.g. banks and *Building societies*) in an economy is to provide means by which funds can be transferred from surplus units (for example, someone with savings to invest in the economy) to deficit units (for example, someone who wants to borrow money to buy a house).

Financial Ombudsman Service (FOS). The FOS offers an informal method of independent adjudication of disputes between a firm and its customer, which is relatively cheap compared with the alternative of taking action through the Courts. The FOS is a body set up by statute and, while its board is appointed by the *FSA*, it is independent from the FSA and authorised firms. The FOS is, however, accountable to the FSA and is required to make an annual report to the FSA on its activities. A complainant must first go to the authorised firm against which the complaint is being made. If the authorised firm does not resolve the complaint to his satisfaction, the complainant may refer it to the FOS.

Financial promotion. The term under *FSMA 2000* for an invitation or inducement to engage in investment activity, such as an advertisement. The term describes most forms and methods of marketing financial services. It covers traditional advertising, most website content, telephone sales campaigns and face-to-face meetings. The term is extended to cover marketing communications by *MiFID*. The purpose of regulation in this area is to create a regime where the quality of financial promotions is scrutinised by an authorised firm who must then comply with lengthy rules to ensure that their promotions are clear, fair and not misleading (Principle 7) and that customers are treated fairly (Principle 6). S21 FSMA 2000 makes it criminal for someone to undertake a financial promotion unless they are either an authorised firm (i.e. issuing the financial promotion), or the content of the communication is approved by an authorised firm.

Financial Reporting Council (FRC). The body that provides the strategic direction behind the development of *Accounting standards* in the UK. It owns two subsidiary companies, the *Accounting Standards Board* and the *Financial Reporting Review Panel*, which issue and enforce accounting standards in the UK.

Financial Reporting Review Panel. The body responsible for ensuring that companies in the UK follow accounting standards. See also *Accounting Standards Board* and *Financial Reporting Council*.

Financial resources. A conservative measure of the capital of an *FSA*-authorised firm. *Capital adequacy* rules require that financial resources must at all times exceed the financial resources requirement.

Financial Services Action Plan (FSAP). As part of a co-ordinated approach to the creation of a single market in Europe, the FSAP was intended to create, originally by 2005, a single market in financial services. The stated aims of the FSAP are to create a single wholesale market, an open and secure retail financial services market and state-of-the-art prudential rules and regulation. The longer-term aim is that Europe will be the world's most competitive economy by 2010.

Financial Services and Markets Act 2000 (FSMA 2000). The Act of Parliament under which the *Financial Services Authority (FSA)* was set up as the UK's statutory regulator of the financial services industry.

Financial Services and Markets Tribunal (FSMT). An independent judicial body established under s132 *FSMA 2000* which hears references arising from decision notices issued by the *FSA*. The decision notices may cover a wide range of regulatory and disciplinary matters and the firm or individual to whom the notice is directed has the right to refer the matter to the FSMT. The Tribunal determines what is the appropriate action for the FSA to take. Decision notices that are referable may cover: authorisation and permission, penalties for market abuse, disciplinary measures, *Official Listing* and other powers (decisions on the approval and discipline of employees and people who carry out certain functions on behalf of authorised persons).

Financial Services Authority (FSA). The regulatory authority for the financial services industry in the UK, set up under *FSMA 2000*.

Financial Services Authority: statutory objectives

- Maintaining confidence in the UK financial system
- Promoting public understanding of the UK financial system
- Securing the appropriate degree of protection for consumers
- Reducing financial crime

Financial Services Compensation Scheme (FSCS). A scheme set up under *FSMA 2000* and run by the *FSA* to compensate investors if authorised firms default, up to the limits set out in the box below.

Financial Services Compensation Scheme limits applying from 1 October 2007

Protected investments: £48,000 (100% of the first £30,000 and 90% of the next £20,000)
Protected deposits: £35,000 (100% of the first £35,000)
Long-term insurance: 100% of first £2,000, plus 90% of remaining value (unlimited)

Financial statements. The annually presented accounts for an enterprise, including the *Balance sheet*, *Income statement* and *Cash flow statement*, together with related notes and other statements as required by legislation or regulation. See also *Annual report and accounts*.

Financial year. The year for which corporation tax rates apply. It runs from 1 April one year to 31 March next year and is denoted by the year in which it starts. For example, the financial year 2008 starts on 1 April 2008 and ends on 31 March 2009. Contrast this with the *Fiscal year*, which is the tax year for income tax and capital gains tax suffered by individuals.

Firm price. A guaranteed price.

First notice day. For *Futures* contracts where notice of delivery can be given by the seller before expiry of the contract, the first day on which such notice can be given.

Fiscal policy. Government policy on taxation, public borrowing and public spending.

Fiscal year. The tax year by reference to which an individual's personal tax liability for income tax and capital gains tax is calculated. The fiscal year runs from 6 April one year to 5 April the next year and is denoted by both years in which it falls. For example, the fiscal year 2008/2009 starts on 6 April 2008 and ends on 5 April 2009.

Fit and proper test. For someone to obtain *Approved person* status, the *FSA* must be satisfied that the person is 'fit and proper' to carry out the controlled function they seek approval for. The test is set out in the *FSA Handbook* in the Fit and Proper Test for Approved Persons Sourcebook (FIT). The most important considerations are: honesty, integrity and reputation; competence and capability; and financial soundness.

Fixed assets. See *Non-current assets*.

Fixed charge. See *Charge*.

Fixed price offer. A method of implementing an *Offer for subscription* or an *Offer for sale*. When a company is issuing shares, it will invite applications for shares at a predetermined price under a fixed price offer. This eliminates uncertainty for investors and the company as to the price that will be set for the issue. A disadvantage is that it can be difficult to identify an appropriate price at which to sell the issue. Alternative approaches include a *Tender offer* and *Bookbuilding*.

Fixed price re-offer. A means of issuing *Eurobonds* where the lead manager of the issue distributes the bonds to the management group who then place the bonds on with their clients. They are not, however, permitted to place the bonds at a price below the fixed price agreed in advance until the syndicate is broken. The syndicate is only broken by the lead manager when most of the issue has been placed at the fixed price. The purpose of this rule is to ensure that when managers bid to participate in the management group, they bid at prices that are realistic. See also *Bought deal*.

Flat yield. The annual gross *Coupon* on a *Bond* divided by its price, expressed as a percentage. For example, a bond with a 10% coupon and a price of 95 has a flat yield of 10 ÷ 95 = 10.5%. Also known as the income yield or the running yield.

Flex (contract). A *Derivatives* contract traded on an exchange where the contract specification allows certain terms of the contract to be negotiated between buyer and seller, unlike a normal standardised derivative contract, where only the price is negotiated. Flexible terms may include *Maturity*, *Strike price* and *Exercise style* of the contract.

Floating charge. See *Charge*.

Floating rate. A rate of interest that varies over time, depending on market rates of interest.

Floating rate note (FRN). A bond that pays a floating rate of interest. The *Interest rate* payable on the bond will be reset at regular intervals, for example each three months or six months.

Footsie. A popular name for the *FTSE 100 Index*.

Forex (or FX). Trading in currencies, i.e. foreign exchange.

Forward rate. The *Exchange rate* agreed on a particular date for a currency transaction to be settled on an agreed date in the future. The difference between the forward rate and the spot rate is determined by the difference in interest rates of the two countries concerned: if it were not, *Arbitrage* would be possible.

Forward Rate Agreement (FRA). A contract between counterparties for a fixed interest rate on a notional principal sum with a specified value date (start date) and *Maturity* (end date). Note that, as with an *Interest rate swap*, there is no exchange of principal. Rather, this is an agreed notional sum on which the contract is based, and compensation is paid or received if the *Interest rate* at the value date differs from the contracted FRA rate.

Free delivery (or 'free of payment'). A *Settlement* situation whereby one side of the trade is delivered in the absence of the other side. If stock changes hands first and then the cash, or *vice versa*, there is a risk that the counterparty might default after the cash has been delivered but before the stock is received. This situation contracts with *Delivery versus payment (DvP)*.

Free float. The proportion of the shares of a public company that are freely available for trading and thus are not subject to sale restrictions.

Free issue. See *Bonus issue*.

Free trade area (or free trade zone). A grouping of countries which has agreed to have no tariffs, quotas or other trade restrictions on trade between its members. Unlike members of a *Customs union*, members of a free trade area may adopt different policies on trade with non-members.

FRN. See *Floating rate note*.

FSA. See *Financial Services Authority*.

FSA Handbook. The final (but continually evolving) set of rules, principles and guidance to which FSA-authorised firms must adhere, including for example the *Principles for Businesses* and the *Conduct of Business rules*. The FSA *Handbook* is split into a number of blocks. Within each block are a number of Sourcebooks. The *Handbook* includes a Glossary of Definitions. The full text of the FSA *Handbook* is available at the FSA's website www.fsa.gov.uk.

FSA Handbook structure

High Level Standards			
Principles for Businesses (PRIN)	Fit and Proper Test for Approved Persons (FIT)	Threshold Conditions (COND)	Fees Manual (FEES)
Statements of Principle and Code of Practice for Approved Persons (APER)	Senior Management Arrangements, Systems and Controls (SYSC)	General Provisions (GEN)	

Prudential Standards

General Prudential Sourcebook (GENPRU)		Prudential Sourcebook for UCITS Firms (UPRU)	Prudential Sourcebook for Mortgage and Home Finance Firms and Insurance Intermediaries (MIPRU)
Prudential Sourcebook for Banks, Building Societies and Investment Firms (BIPRU)	Prudential Sourcebook for Insurers (INSPRU)		

Interim Prudential Sourcebooks (IPRU):				
▪ Banks	▪ Building Societies	▪ Friendly Societies	▪ Insurers	▪ Investment businesses

Business Standards

Conduct of Business (COBS)	Insurance: Conduct of Business (ICOB)	Mortgages: Conduct of Business (MCOB)
Client Assets (CASS)	Training and Competence (TC)	Market Conduct (MAR)

Regulatory Processes

Supervision Manual (SUP)	Decision Procedure and Penalties Manual (DEPP)

Redress

Dispute Resolution: Complaints (DISP)	Compensation (COMP)	Complaints Against the FSA (COAF)

Specialist Sourcebooks

Collective Investment Schemes (COLL)	Electronic Money (ELM)	
Professional Firms (PROF)	Credit Unions (CRED)	Recognised Investment Exchanges/ Clearing Houses (REC)

Listing Prospectus and Disclosure

Listing Rules (LR)	Prospectus Rules (PR)	Disclosure Rules and Transparency Rules (DTR)

Icons in the FSA *Handbook*	
R	*Rule*
E	*Evidential provision*
G	*Guidance*
C	*Conclusive provision*
D	The 'D' icon indicates a direction, which is binding on the persons or categories of person to whom it is addressed.
P	'P' is used for *Statements of Principle for Approved Persons*.
EU	'EU' (or the EU flag) is used to indicate non-FSA EU legislative material, such as EU Directives and directly applicable EU Regulations.
UK	'UK' (or the UK flag) indicates directly applicable non-FSA UK legislative material, such as Acts of Parliament and statutory instruments, regulations and orders.

FSAP. See *Financial Services Action Plan*.

FSMA 2000. See *Financial Services and Markets Act 2000*.

FT 30 Index (also known as the FT Ordinary Share Index). The oldest UK share price index established in 1935 by the *Financial Times* with a base value of 100 and reflecting the share prices of 30 of the largest companies in the UK. The FT 30 is an unweighted index with each share counting equally rather than in proportion to its market capitalisation. It is calculated a a geometric mean. Rather than qualifying on the basis of size, companies are included in the FT 30 by discretion of the committee that compiles the index, so as to reflect a wide range c sectors in the economy. This selection procedure is similar to that used for the *Dow Jone Industrial Average*. The FT 30 is rarely quoted nowadays as a barometer of the market although it might be of some use to economists as its constituents widely represent differen industrial, commercial and service sectors.

FT Ordinary Share Index. An alternative name for the *FT30 Index*.

FTSE 100 Index (the 'Footsie'). The Financial Times Stock Exchange 100 Index (the 'Footsie is the best-known UK share price index and is the index most often quoted as the 'baromete for the share market. The FTSE 100 is capitalisation-weighted and comprises the shares of th 100 UK companies with the largest market capitalisation. Constituent reviews of the companie in the index are carried out quarterly. Additions and deletions are performed strictly accordance with a set of rules supervised by an independent Steering Committee. The bas date of the index was 1 January 1984, when the base number was 1,000. An index based c 100 companies may not initially seem very comprehensive but, given the size of th companies included, the FTSE 100 Index represents approximately 80% of the tot capitalisation of the UK equity market.

FTSE 250 Index. A capitalisation-weighted share price index comprised of the next 250 companies after the FTSE 100 companies by market capitalisation (i.e. the 101st largest company to the 350th largest). The FTSE 250 represents approximately 18% of the total UK market capitalisation. The constituent companies are reviewed quarterly. A version of the FTSE 250 excluding investment trusts is published.

FTSE 350 Index. A share price index which is a combination of the *FTSE 100 Index* and the *FTSE 250 Index* and so covers the UK's top 350 companies by market capitalisation. There are three variations on this index, one of which is the index excluding investment trusts. The other two variants are on the basis of yield. The constituent companies are ranked according to dividend yield and divided in two to produce separate higher yield and lower yield indices.

FTSE AIM Index Series. A set of share price indices covering companies on the *Alternative Investment Market (AIM)*. The FTSE AIM Series comprises the following real-time indices: FTSE AIM UK 50 Index (largest 50 eligible UK companies), FTSE AIM 100 Index (largest 100 eligible companies), FTSE AIM All-Share Index (comprising all AIM companies meeting criteria for liquidity and *Free float*).

FTSE All-Share Index. A capitalisation-weighted share price index made up of approximately 800 shares of more than 2,000 listed UK companies. The companies in the All-Share Index represent around 98% of the total capitalisation of the UK equity market. Constituent companies are reviewed annually in December. As with other indices, there is a version that excludes investment trusts. The All-Share Index is less affected by price movements in individual shares than the FTSE 100 Index and this makes it a useful index for a tracker fund. As a *Benchmark*, the All-Share provides the widest representation of a diversified UK share portfolio. The All-Share Index is divided into 38 sectors covering the various sectors in which UK companies operate. The FTSE All-Share is an aggregation of the FTSE 100, FTSE 250 and FTSE Small Cap indices (see diagram below).

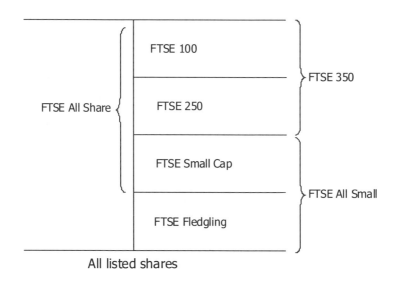

All listed shares

FTSE All-Small Index. A share price index combining the *FTSE Small Cap Index* and the *FTSE Fledgling Index*. The All-Small index is calculated at the daily close of business and is reviewed annually in December.

FTSE Eurotop 100. A share price index comprising the 100 highest capitalisation *Blue chip* shares in Europe (including the UK).

FTSE Fledgling Index. A share price index made up of around 300 companies that are smaller in size than those in the *FTSE Small Cap Index*. The FTSE Fledgling Index represents approximately one per cent of UK market capitalisation. There is a version of the Fledgling Index that excludes investment trusts. The Fledgling Index is calculated at the end of each trading day, and a review of constituent companies is held annually in December.

FTSE Small Cap Index. A share price index comprised of companies with the smallest capitalisation of the capital and industry segments of the *FTSE All-Share Index*, by excluding *FTSE 350 Index* constituents from the All-Share Index. The FTSE Small Cap Index represents approximately two per cent of the total UK market capitalisation and there is a variant that excludes investment trusts. A review of constituent companies is carried out quarterly.

FTSE techMARK indices. TechMARK is a sector comprising businesses at the cutting edge of technological innovation. The FTSE techMARK All-Share Index includes all TechMARK companies that are in the *FTSE All-Share Index*. The top 100 of these shares make up the FTSE techMARK 100 Index. There is also a FTSE techMARK mediscience Index including pharmaceutical, biotechnology and medical equipment and supplies companies.

FTSE4Good indices. A range of ethical or *SRI* share price indices designed to identify and measure the performance of companies working towards environmental sustainability, positive relationships with stakeholders, and upholding and supporting universal human rights. The establishment of the FTSE4Good indices follows earlier development in the USA of the Dow Jones Sustainability Group Indices. FTSE4Good indices comprise indices for the UK, for Europe for the USA, and for global investing.

Full replication. A *Passive fund management* whereby the fund attempts to mirror the index by holding shares in exactly the same proportions as in the index itself. Contrast with *Stratified sampling*.

Fully diluted earnings per share. A notional calculation designed to warn shareholders of potential deterioration of *Earnings per share* in the future as a result of new shares being issued by the company on the exercise of *Convertible debt, Warrants* or *Options* already in issue. The calculation reworks the *Earnings per share* figure for the current year on the basis that the dilution had already occurred, as if the *Exercise* of the convertibles (etc) had already taken place.

Fund. A term used to describe types of *Collective investment scheme*, which are vehicles which investors' monies are pooled together and managed as a single entity with a common investment aim. *Unit trusts* and *Open-ended Investment Companies (OEICs)* are together referred to as 'funds'.

Funds: Investment Management Association sector classifications

Income funds		Growth funds		Specialist funds
Immediate income	**Growing income**	**Capital protection**	**Capital growth/total return**	
UK Gilts UK Index Linked Gilts UK Corporate Bond UK Other Bond Global Bonds UK Equity & Bond Income	UK Equity Income	Money Market Protected/ Guaranteed Funds	UK All Companies UK Smaller Companies Japan Japanese Smaller Companies Asia Pacific including Japan Asia Pacific excluding Japan North America North American Smaller Companies Europe including UK Europe excluding UK European Smaller Companies Cautious Managed Balanced Managed Active Managed Global Growth Global Emerging Markets UK Zeros	Specialist Technology & Telecomm-unications Personal Pensions

Fund of funds. A *Fund* packages together and invests in a number of funds. The investor may be subject to a double layer of charges with such an arrangement.

Fundamental analysis. For corporate securities, fundamental analysis involves economic analysis of markets in which a company operates and analysis of published corporate information with a view to forecasting future profits and determining fair values and hence, the potential for mis-pricing. A basic idea behind this analytical approach is that a security has an intrinsic value that can be determined from a consideration of these factors. With government bonds, this form of analysis entails reviewing the economic outlook for the economy and the funding requirement. Contrast with *Technical analysis*.

Funeral plan contracts. An investment whereby a person makes payments during their lifetime to pay for their funeral expenses upon death.

Future. A standardised contract to buy or sell a standard quantity of a specified asset for delivery at a fixed future date at a price agreed today. Futures are traded on futures exchanges, such as *Euronext.liffe*, the *London Metal Exchange* and *ICE Futures*. Futures are available in a range of assets, for example wheat and copper, and also on indices, such as the *FTSE 100 Index*.

Future value. See *Terminal value*.

FX (or forex). Trading in currencies, i.e. foreign exchange.

G

GAAP. See *Generally Accepted Account Principles*.

Gamma. In respect of *Options* and *Futures*, the rate of change of *Delta* with respect to the price of the underlying. Gamma indicates how fast an option's position is becoming increasingly or decreasingly *Bullish* or *Bearish*.

GBP. Pounds sterling (£).

GBX. Pence sterling (£).

GCM. See *General clearing member*.

GD. Good for the Day – an order type, such that the order must be filled during the day otherwise it is cancelled. Contrast with a *GTC* (Good 'Til Cancelled) order which, if not filled on one trading day, is carried forward indefinitely until it is either filled or cancelled by the investor. Orders are generally treated as GD unless otherwise specified.

GDR. See *Global Depository Receipt*.

Gearing (or leverage). The situation when an asset is controlled for a relatively low up-front cost. The impact is that profits or losses on the position are magnified in percentage terms. This can be achieved by financial gearing, where an investor borrows money to buy an asset, thus reducing the initial cash outlay required. Alternatively, *Futures* and *Options* can be used to create gearing. In the case of futures, the investor only has to pay upfront *Margin* when buying futures contracts rather than paying the whole purchase price. In the case of options, the investor only has to pay an upfront premium. In the case of companies, their level of financial gearing is measured by the *Gearing ratio* and *Interest cover*.

Gearing ratio. An accounting ratio which measures the level of debt finance a company has raised relative to its level of *Shareholders' funds*, also known as the debt/equity ratio. The ratio is usually (but not always) defined as interest-bearing debt divided by shareholder funds, expressed as a percentage. The higher the percentage, the more highly geared company is. It is possible to calculate the net gearing ratio, where cash balances are deducted from debt in the calculation.

GEMM. See *Gilt-Edged Market Maker*.

General clearing member. A *Clearing member* of a clearing house who has the capacity clear for the firm, its clients and other investment businesses. Contrast with *Individual clearing members*, who can clear for the firm and its clients only, not for other investment businesses.

General client account. A *Client money* bank account for segregated customers. The accounts, unlike *Designated client accounts*, may be pooled upon default.

General prohibition. The requirement that persons carrying out a regulated activity in the UK by way of business must either be authorised by the FSA or granted exemption, as required by section 19 of *FSMA 2000*.

Generally Accepted Accounting Principles. The acronym GAAP is used for Generally Accepted Accounting Principles, which differ to some degree for the UK and internationally – see below, and see *Accounting standards*.

Generally Accepted Accounting Principles – differences in terminology

UK GAAP	International GAAP
Balance sheet	Balance sheet
Profit and loss account	Income statement
Cash flow statement	Cash flow statement
Statement of total recognised gains and losses (STRGL)	Changes in equity or statement of total recognised income and expenses (SORIE)
Historical cost profit	N/a
Accounting policies	Accounting policies
Notes to the accounts	Notes to the accounts
Fixed assets	Non-current assets
Tangible fixed assets	Property, plant and equipment
Trade debtors	Trade receivables
Trade creditors	Trade payables
Stock	Inventory
Turnover	Revenue
Reserves	Reserves
Depreciation/Amortisation	Depreciation/Amortisation
Profit and loss reserve	Retained earnings

Gift Aid. An evidenced donation to charity that is an allowable deduction from gross income for income tax.

Gift *inter vivos* policy. A decreasing term assurance policy specifically designed to cover the potential *Inheritance tax* liability in the seven-year period after someone makes a *Potentially Exempt Transfer (PET)*.

Gilt-Edged Market Maker (GEMM). An *LSE* member firm which is obliged to quote firm two-way prices, i.e. guaranteed prices at which they will buy and sell, for all conventional gilts or all index-linked gilts. In the latter case, the market maker is known as an IG GEMM.

Gilt-edged securities (also known simply as *'Gilts'*). Bonds (excluding *Treasury bills*) issued by the UK Government through the *Debt Management Office*. Capital gains and losses arising on disposal of gilts are exempt from capital gains tax. The two main types are conventional gilts and *Index-linked gilts*.

Gilts. A term used for *Gilt-edged securities*.

GIPS. See *Global Investment Performance Standards*.

Give ups. See *Allocation*.

Global Depository Receipts (GDRs). Certificates issued by a bank in more than country and representing ownership of securities in a foreign company. These are similar to *American Depository Receipts (ADRs)*.

Global Investment Performance Standards (GIPS). A set of ethical standards established by the *CFA Institute* that enable investment managers to present and disclose investment performance in a way that is accepted and acknowledged globally. Institutional investors particularly use performance as a critical criterion in selecting investment managers. The GIPS allow investors to compare investment performance using a consistent methodology with the objective of enhancing professionalism of the industry.

GLOBEX. A screen trading system developed by the *CME* and the quote vendor, Reuters CME, *CBOT* and *Euronext* Paris products trade upon it.

Going concern concept. A concept underlying the preparation of *Financial statements* which involves the assumption that the business will continue in operational existence for the foreseeable future. The going concern concept assumes that the business will be able to realise assets and to discharge liabilities in the normal course of its business. If this assumption does not apply – for example, if the business is soon to be closed down – then different approach might need to be taken to valuing assets and liabilities of the business. The business may be forced to sell assets at relatively low prices, and there could be costs in winding-up the business which ought to be allowed for in the accounts.

Gold plating. In European regulation, the addition by Member States of their own rules in the process of implementing European Directives. Gold plating is considered contrary to the principle of 'maximum harmonisation' but is permitted in some cases on a basis called *'Superequivalence'*. Article 4 of the *MiFID* Implementing Directive allows superequivalence where it can be justified and is proportionate in addressing specific risks.

Goodwill. The difference between the total value of a business and the value of its net asset in the *Balance sheet*.

Grantor. An LME term for an options *Writer*.

Gratis issue. See *Bonus issue*.

Greenshoe option. A means of stabilising a new issue. The manager of the issue will sell more shares under the offer for sale than the actual number of new shares being created. This short position in the stock is covered by an *Option* on new shares to be issued by the company. If the share price after the issue rises above the *Exercise price* of the option, the manager can close his position by exercising the option on the company. This enables the company to access the market for additional funds on the issue. If the share price falls below the exercise price of the option, the manager will let the option lapse and close his position by buying shares in the market. This will create additional demand for the shares and act as a stabilising mechanism.

Grey market. Trading in a Bond prior to the formal issue of the bond. Trading is completed on an 'if, as and when issued' basis. *Settlement* takes place when the bond is finally issued.

Gross domestic product (GDP). The value of the goods and services produced by an economy in a given period.

Gross national income. GDP *plus* income accruing to domestic residents from investments abroad *less* income accruing to foreign residents from investments in the domestic economy.

Gross redemption yield (GRY). The total return on a *Bond*, taking into account both coupon and the capital gain or loss on maturity. Under the Japanese method, it is calculated as the flat yield of the bond plus any capital gain on redemption (less any capital loss), where the capital gain or loss is divided by the number of years to maturity and expressed as a percentage of the current bond price, i.e.:

[(Gross coupon ÷ Market price) + ({Par - Market price} ÷ No. of years to redemption) ÷ Market price] × 100%

The above Japanese method ignores the time value of money. In practice, an appropriate discount factor must be applied to future cash flows. Thus, a more accurate gross redemption yield is the interest rate that discounts all future cash flows on a bond and sums them to the current market value of the bond. It is also known as the yield to maturity.

GTC (Good 'Til Cancelled). An order type such that, if the order is not filled on the day it was received, it is carried forward indefinitely until it is either traded or cancelled by the customer. Contrast with a *GD* (Good for the Day) order, where the order must be filled the same day or is cancelled.

Guarantee fund contributions. Contributions made to a guarantee fund by the *Clearing members* of a clearing house operating a mutual guarantee. The guarantee fund will be used in the event of a *Default* of a clearing member causing losses, and must be exhausted before the resources of the clearing house are then used.

Guarantee stock. A *Bond* where the lender's performance of its obligations is guaranteed by a third party. These often arise where a subsidiary company raises external finance and the bond is guaranteed by its holding company.

Guaranteed fund. A *Fund* that promises to return at least the original sum invested to the investor after a set period (normally five to seven years) and, in addition, further profits if the fund has traded successfully.

Guaranteed stop. An order type where the investor is guaranteed that the stop order will be filled at the stop level specified and not the prevailing market price when the stop is filled. Such an order involves large risks for the broker, and therefore such orders are rare and incur high charges.

Guidance. In the *FSA Handbook*, guidance – indicated by the letter 'G' – is used to flesh out particular issues arising from rules. Guidance is not binding on a firm and it need not be followed in order to achieve compliance with the relevant rule. Accordingly, if a firm fails to act in accordance with guidance, there is no presumption that the linked rule has been breached. However, if a firm acts in accordance with guidance, then the FSA will proceed on the assumption that it has followed the linked rule.

Haircut. A name for the discounting of collateral given to the *LCH.Clearnet* to cover *Initial margin* payments. This means that the value given to the collateral by LCH will be less than its current market value, the difference between the two sums being the haircut. This protects the clearing house by taking into account the lesser value that it is likely to get in the event of a forced sale of the collateral to meet losses caused by a clearing member default.

Hang Seng Index. An index of share prices for major Hong Kong Stock companies, weighted by *Market capitalisation*. The 40 companies included represent around 65% of the capitalisation of the Hong Kong Stock Exchange.

Hard commodities. *Commodities* that need to be extracted (mined or drilled) from the ground. Hard commodities include energy products, metals (gold, copper, lead, tin, nickel, uranium etc) and diamonds, which all generally require substantial capital expenditure to extract. These commodities are finite resources. See also *Soft commodities*.

Hawala. In Islamic finance, the transfer of money from one person to another. The recipient may make administrative charges, which should not be proportionate to the sum of money.

Headroom. The difference between a *CREST* member's cap, i.e. the credit they have available, and the net *Cash Memorandum Account (CMA)* balance, i.e. the cash movements from that day's activities.

Hedge. A transaction whose objective is to reduce *Risk*. For example, a wheat farmer may sell wheat *Futures* (i.e. a short hedge) to guarantee him a fixed selling price for his wheat.

Hedge fund. A type of fund, often based offshore and generally targeted at *High net worth individuals*, which uses a variety of investment strategies, which may for example include taking short positions, to enhance investment returns. The charging structure often provides substantial performance incentives to the hedge fund manager.

Her Majesty's Revenue & Customs (HMRC). The name for the amalgamated Inland Revenue and HM Customs & Excise.

Her Majesty's Treasury (HMT). See *HM Treasury*.

Herstatt risk. A term for overnight delivery risk named after the Herstatt Bank (Bankhaus Herstatt), which was closed during the day in Germany by the Bundesbank on 16 June 1974 after *FX* losses. This left many who had dealt with Herstatt Bank with significant exposures due to the timing of clearing and settlement arrangements. These banks had paid out Deutschmarks to Herstatt Bank but the closure prevented them receiving US dollars in return. Overnight delivery risks from this kind of default are thus often known as Herstatt risk.

Higgs Report. In response to concerns surrounding high profile scandals in the US (notably Enron and WorldCom), Derek Higgs was asked to review the role of the non-executive directors of listed companies in the UK. His report, published in 2003, advocated greater meritocracy in appointing non-executives.

High Level Standards. A term used to collectively describe the *Principles for Businesses* and *Statements of Principle* and the rest of Block 1 of the FSA *Handbook*.

High net worth individual. Sometimes defined as someone with at least US $1,000,000 in liquid assets.

High yielding bond. An alternative term for a *Junk bond*.

Highly Leveraged Transaction (HLT). See *Leveraged buyout*.

Historic volatility. The volatility of the price of an asset during a past period. This can be used by a trader to forecast future volatility of the price.

HMRC. See *Her Majesty's Revenue & Customs*.

HM Treasury (HMT). The UK Government department responsible, among other things, for implementing *FSMA 2000*.

Holding company. A company that controls one or more *Subsidiary companies* in which it owns shares.

Horizontal spread. An option spread where one option is purchased and a different option is sold. The sold option has the same *Strike price* but a different *Expiry* date from the purchased option. The spread will be constructed with either all calls or all puts on the same *Underlying asset*. This spread is sometimes known as a time spread or a calendar spread.

Hybrid. A security, such as a convertible debt instrument, that has characteristics of both *Bond* and an equity instrument.

ICE Futures (formerly the International Petroleum Exchange (IPE)). An electronic regulated *Futures* and *Options* exchange for global energy markets. ICE's trading platform offers participants access to a wide range of energy futures products. Contracts include the Brent global crude benchmark contract, gas oil, natural gas, electricity, and ECX carbon financial instruments, until the name was changed in 2005. The IPE was established in 1980 when it started trading Gas Oil futures. The exchange was acquired by the IntercontinentalExchange (ICE®) of Atlanta, Georgia in 2001. ICE is one of the world's largest electronic commodity and energy trading groups. All contracts are traded electronically using ICE's system known as The Interchange™. ICE operates global market places for the trading of energy commodity futures and OTC contracts on its Internet-based Interchange™ trading platform.

ICM. See *Individual clearing member*.

ICMA. See *International Capital Market Association (ICMA)*.

ICVC. See *Investment company with variable capital*.

IDB. See *Inter-dealer broker*.

Idiosyncratic risk. See *Unsystematic risk*.

IDRs. See *International Depository Receipts*.

If as and when issued. See *Grey market*.

IFA. See *Independent Financial Adviser*.

IFRSs. See *International Financial Reporting Standards*.

IG GEMM. See *Gilt-Edged Market Maker*.

Ijara. In Islamic finance, a form of leasing where the bank buys an item and then leases it to a customer for a pre-agreed rental over a specific period.

Ijara wa iqtana. In Islamic finance, a contract similar to *Ijara* but including a promise from the customer to buy the item at the end of the lease period, often for a token amount.

ILG. See *Index-linked gilts*.

Illiquid. The term for an investment that is difficult to sell. Unlisted securities and Over-The-Counter products are relatively illiquid. See also *Liquidity*.

IMA. See *Investment Management Association*.

Immunisation. The process where it is possible to create a portfolio that will provide an assured return over a specific time horizon irrespective of any changes in the interest rate. Therefore, if we need to match a liability, we should select a *Bond* portfolio with the same *Duration* as the liability it is intended to meet.

Implied volatility. In relation to options, the market's perception as to future volatility can be implied by the input of the market price of an option into the theoretical option pricing model, along with the other known inputs, namely time to *Expiry*, *Exercise price*, *Underlying asset* price and *Interest rates* in order to find the unknown volatility.

IMS. See *Interim management statement*.

In-the-money. An *Option* or *Warrant* is said to be 'in-the-money' when it has *Intrinsic value*. For a *Call option* or a *Warrant*, this is when the price of the *Underlying asset* exceeds the *Exercise price* of the option. For example, a call option on a share with an exercise price of 100p when the share price is 110p is in-the-money. For a *Put option*, it is when the exercise price exceeds the asset price. For example, a put option on a share with an exercise price of 100p when the share price is 90p is in-the-money. See also *At-the-money* and *Out-of-the-money*.

Income Protection Insurance (IPI*)*. A type of insurance that provides replacement of income in the event that the insured is unable to work for a prolonged period of time. IPI is sometimes known by its former name 'Permanent Health Insurance' ('PHI').

Income statement. The part of a company's *Financial statements* providing an analysis of how the company has generated its profit or loss for the accounting period. The income statement helps to explain why the *Balance sheet* has changed from one period to the next.

Income yield. See *Flat yield*.

Independence policy (policy of independence). A written policy used by certain *FSA* firms to manage *Conflicts of interest*. A policy of independence, which must be made known to private customers, requires that the firm and its employees disregard the firm's interests. See also *Chinese walls*.

Independent Financial Adviser (IFA). An adviser in the retail financial services market who offers advice on all the products in the market or in a whole market sector. Contrast with *Appointed representative* and *Multi-tied adviser*.

Independent guarantee. A type of guarantee operated by clearing houses where losses caused by *Clearing member* defaults are covered initially from the defaulting clearing member's assets (if any), and then from the clearing house's own resources. There is no guarantee fund contributed to by the clearing members with this type of guarantee, unlike the *Mutual guarantee* where such a fund exists.

Index-linked gilts. *Gilts* where the coupon payments and capital redemption value are linked to the increase in the *Retail Prices Index (RPI)* over the period the bond has been issue, thus giving *Inflation* protection to investors. The bigger the increase in the RPI, the higher the value of the coupon and the capital value.

Indexation allowance. The calculation that reduces the profit on disposal for capital gains tax purposes by allowing for inflation over the period when the asset was owned. The calculation is based on the cost of buying the asset multiplied by the proportional increase in the *RPI* over the period the asset was owned. Indexation can be used to reduce a gain, but cannot be used to convert a pre-indexation gain into a post-indexation loss or to increase a pre-indexation loss. It is given from the date purchased (or 31 March 1982 if later) through to 6 April 1998. The part of the gain after April 1998 is reduced by *Taper relief.*

Index tracker fund. A fund that passive tracks an index: see *Passive fund management.*

Indirect quote. In the *Forex (FX)* markets, an *Exchange rate* expressed in foreign currency per unit of the domestic currency. The opposite of a *Direct quote*.

Individual clearing member. A *Clearing member* of a clearing house who has the capacity to clear for the firm and its clients only. Contrast with *General clearing members*, who can clear for the firm, its clients and other investment businesses.

Individual Savings Account (ISA). A savings 'wrapper' that allows UK investors to hold certain shares, life insurance products and *Stakeholder products* free of income and capital gains tax.

Individual Vetting and Registration Department. A department of the *FSA* that deals with applications for *Approved person* status.

Inflation. An increase in price levels generally. The *Consumer Price Index (CPI)* and the *Retail Prices Index (RPI)* are key measures of consumer price inflation in the UK.

Information risk. See *Reporting risk.*

Information society service. A service provided: electronically, e.g. via the Internet or e-mail; at a distance, i.e. cross border: it does not cover setting up branches; for remuneration; and at the request of the individual: this means it will not cover unsolicited approaches. For example, the definition would cover online dealing, trading services and cross-border marketing activities other than unsolicited marketing.

Infrastructure fund. A fund providing private finance for infrastructure projects such as roads, railways, seaports, airports and tunnels. Finance for infrastructure investment has traditionally been an area mainly for the wholesale market, because such investments are Illiquid and not divisible into small units. A typical project involves large capital outlay, often with a long payback period. More recently, there has been success in providing infrastructure funds in the retail market, offered by managers who package them into a listed vehicle.

Inheritance tax. Tax payable on the worldwide chargeable estate of a UK-domiciled individual on death.

Initial capital requirement. A minimum level of resources that a firm must exceed when first seeking authorisation by the *FSA*.

Initial Disclosure Document (IDD). In relation to *Packaged products* business, the document covering 'Key Facts: About our Services' for disclosure to a *Retail client* by a firm in a *Durable medium* on making initial contact or 'in good time' before the client is bound by an agreement to provide advice or the firm performs an act preparatory to providing advice. The Combined IDD is for cases where home finance as well as other business is being provided. The IDD and Combined IDD contain the 'keyfacts' logo, and specified headings and text. See also *Menu*.

Initial margin. The returnable deposit required by clearing houses when opening certain futures and options positions. Initial margin is usually calculated by taking the worst probable one-day loss that the position could sustain, and can be paid in either cash or collateral.

Initial Public Offering (IPO). A share issue, when a company comes to the market for the first time and offers its shares to the public.

Injunction. A Court order prohibiting a party from performing or continuing to perform a specific course of action.

Insider dealing. A criminal offence under the Criminal Justice Act 1993 of carrying out certain activities while possessing price-sensitive information that is not publicly available. The following activities are offences when undertaken by an insider: dealing in price-affected securities on the basis of inside information, encouraging another person to do so, or disclosing the inside information, unless no dealing is expected. The maximum penalty is seven years' imprisonment and an unlimited fine.

Insider list. A list of persons, whether they are employees or not, with access to inside information about the issuer, which issuers of financial instruments are required to set up by the Disclosure Rules and Transparency Rules (DTR 2.8). The list must be provided to the *FSA* on request and must show each person's identity, the reason for the person being on the list and the date of creation and updating of the list.

Instant auction. An order-driven system where buy and sell orders are instantly matched by the system if the prices at which the buyer and seller are prepared to deal match up. A system of trading used on *virt-x*, also known as continuous auction or automatic matching.

Institutional Shareholders Committee (ISC). A forum which allows the UK's institutional shareholding community to exchange views and, on occasion, to co-ordinate their activities in support of the interests of UK investors. ISC constituent members are the Association of British Insurers (ABI), the Association of Investment Companies (AIC), the Investment Management Association (IMA), and the National Association of Pension Funds (NAPF). The ISC's Statement of Principles on the Responsibilities of Institutional Shareholders and Agents, first published in 2002 and subsequently updated, develops its earlier principles and expands on the *Combined Code on Corporate Governance*.

Intangibles. In the *Balance sheet* of a company, *Non-current assets* that are not physical e.g. goodwill and brands.

Integration. In *Money laundering*, the process of re-using funds in legitimate activity, once steps have been taken to conceal the ownership or origin of the funds. Other phases in the laundering of money are *Placement* and *Layering*.

Intended settlement date (or settlement due date). The date on which payment is due for a trade.

Inter-Dealer Broker (IDB). Stock Exchange member firm who acts as intermediaries for anonymous trading between *Market makers*. When a market maker wishes to complete a large trade, he may advertise the trade through an IDB. Another market maker may take the other side of the bargain. The deal is anonymous, with neither market maker knowing who is completing the other side of the trade. This is achieved by having the market makers dealing with the IDB as a *Principal*, rather than as an *Agent* between the two final participants. They can be divided into Gilt IDBs (who only deal with *GEMMs*), wholesale dealer brokers (who deal in gilts with anyone) and Equity IDBs (who deal in equities with anyone).

Interest accrual. Interest earned but not yet paid, for example on a *Bond*. When a bond is sold, the purchaser will have to compensate the seller for interest accrued up to the date of sale. This is achieved by means of adding on an interest accrual to the *Clean price* being quoted in the market, to give the *Dirty price* payable by the purchaser.

Interest cover. An accounting ratio measuring the level of a company's profits relative to its interest charge in the *Income statement* (profit and loss account). It is usually defined as profits before interest and tax divided by interest charges, but the precise definition will vary depending on the circumstances. The higher the ratio, the less *Gearing* a company has.

Interest rate. The price charged by a lender to a borrower for the use of money, often expressed as an annual percentage of the amount loaned.

Interest rate risk. The variability in return caused by changes in the level of prevailing *Interest rates*.

Interest rate swap. An agreement to pay or receive a sum of money calculated by reference to the difference between two interest payment streams (typically a *Floating rate* of interest and a fixed rate of interest), based on a notional principal sum.

Interim Management Statement (IMS). A requirement under the Companies Act 2006, this is a statement explaining material events and transactions that have taken place since the beginning of the relevant period and their impact on the company's financial position and describing the company's financial position and performance during that time. Companies must publish an IMS during the first six-month period and during the second six-month period of any financial year, unless it produces quarterly financial reports. The IMS must be released between ten weeks after the beginning and six weeks before the end of the relevant six-month period.

Inter-market spread. A transaction involving the purchase of a *Future* on one asset and the sale of a future in another, usually related, asset – e.g. purchasing a Brent crude oil future and selling a gas oil future. Such *Spreads* are entered into in order to profit from a change in the price differential between the two products.

Intermediaries offer. An issue of shares where intermediaries such as brokers and investment banks apply for shares on behalf of their own client base. This is a method of issuing shares used by companies which are obtaining a listing of their shares for the first time.

Internal audit. A department within the enterprise which performs various services for management, including tests of operating, financial and regulatory controls and reviews of operating practices to promote increased efficiency and economy, and which carries out special projects and inquiries at management's discretion. Internal audit reports to management and often to an independent *Audit Committee*.

Internal Capital Adequacy Assessment Process (ICAAP). The process, under Pillar 2 of the *Basel II* provisions, by which a firm is required to assess regularly the amount of internal capital it considers adequate to cover all of the risks to which it is exposed within the context of its overall risk management framework. ICAAP is the firm's responsibility and forms a key input into the *FSA's* supervisory review process.

Internal control. A process set up by the directors of an enterprise which is designed to provide reasonable assurance on the achievement of effective and efficient operations, safeguarding of assets, reliability of financial reporting and compliance with legislation and regulations. For example, see *Preventive controls* and *Segregation of duties*.

Internal rate of return (IRR). The rate of interest that discounts investment flows to a net present value of zero.

International Accounting Standards (IASs). See *International Financial Reporting Standards (IFRSs)*.

International Bank for Reconstruction and Development (IBRD). See *World Bank*.

International Bulletin Board (ITBB). A service introduced by the *LSE* in 2004 that allows registered *Market makers* to support *Liquidity* in equities within a central limit order book structure. ITBB is part of the *International Order Book* (IOB). In 2004, the remainder of the previous *SEAQ* International system was closed down. So today, all *Depository receipts* are traded in the IOB and all equities on ITBB.

International Capital Market Association (ICMA). An association with around 800 members across over 50 countries, formed in 2005 in a merger between the International Securities Markets Association (ISMA), the self-regulatory industry body and trade association for the international securities market, and the International Primary Markets Association (IPMA), the professional association for institutions engaged in primary (new issues) market for international securities. ICMA is recognised by the *FSA* as a *Designated investment exchange* responsible for the market place in international securities such as *Eurobonds*. Trades undertaken are reported into the *TRAX* system.

International Central Securities Depository (ICSD). *Depositories* which have traditionally provided *Clearance* and *Custody* for *Eurobonds* and other *Euromarket* instrument and have increasingly become involved in *Settlement* and *Custody* of international equities. The main ICSDs are *Euroclear* and *Clearstream*.

International Depository Receipts (IDRs). Certificates issued by a bank and representing ownership of securities by an investor outside the security's country of origin. These operate similarly to *American Depository Receipts (ADRs)*.

International Financial Reporting Standards (IFRSs). Together with their predecessors, International Accounting Standards (IASs), IFRSs can be considered to have replaced UK Accounting Standards in the overall context of UK *GAAP* (Generally Accepted Accounting Principles), at least for main-market listed companies. In June 2002, the *EU* adopted a regulation requiring listed companies in Member States (including the UK) to prepare their group/consolidated financial statements using 'adopted International Accounting Standards' for accounting periods beginning on or after 1 January 2005. Companies listed on the *Alternative Investment Market (AIM)* have been required to adopt IFRS for accounting periods beginning on or after 1 January 2007.

International Monetary Fund (IMF). An international organisation with 185 member countries. The IMF was established to promote international monetary co-operation, exchange stability and orderly exchange arrangements; to foster economic growth and high levels of employment; and to provide temporary financial assistance to countries to help ease balance of payments adjustment.

International Order Book (IOB) A platform established by the *LSE* in 2001 for trading in *Depository receipts*, one of the most liquid sectors of overseas securities. The market is based on an electronic order book similar to *SETS* but with the added option for member firms to display their identity pre-trade by using Named Orders, offering greater visibility in the market. The IOB led to strong growth in *Depository Receipt* trading in emerging markets in London, particularly Russia. See also *International Bulletin Board (ITBB)*.

International Organisation of Securities Commissions (IOSCO). An organisation whose aim is to promote high standards of regulation in the international markets to maintain efficient and orderly markets. IOSCO members are national securities regulators and number around 180. Members exchange information in order to develop their own markets and try to establish common standards for their markets. Members also co-ordinate surveillance and enforcement of breaches of market regulation. The IOSCO Principles (established in 1998) are widely recognised as key benchmarks in the standards of good regulation of the securities markets.

International Retail Service (IRS). A service of the *LSE* providing UK retail investors access to trading in international stocks. The service supports trading in major European and US *Blue chips*, using sterling prices generated by *Market makers* (Committed Principals or CPs).

Intestacy. The situation where someone dies without leaving a valid will.

Intraday margin. If a market suddenly becomes highly volatile, a clearing house may call in additional intraday *Margin* payments at short notice in order to reduce the increased risk it would otherwise suffer.

Intra-market spread. A *Futures spread* trade where one delivery month is sold and another bought in the same underlying product, to take advantage of an expected change in price differential between the two delivery months. This could occur, for example, because of short-term supply problems with the near-dated future. See also *Borrowing* and *Carrying*.

Intrinsic value. Used in connection with *Options* and *Warrants*. For a *Call option* or a warrant on shares, it is the amount by which the share price exceeds the *Exercise* price of the option or warrant. For a *Put option*, it is the amount by which the exercise price exceeds the share price, i.e. it is the net amount received if an investor exercises the warrant or option and then closes out the position by buying a share (for a put option) or selling a share (for a call option or a warrant). For example, a call option with an exercise price of 100p when the share price is 150p has intrinsic value of 50p. The holder of the option could exercise the option, buy a share for 100p and then immediately sell the share for 150p, giving a net payoff of 50p. Intrinsic value has a minimum value of zero, since an investor would never exercise an option to give a loss.

Introduction. A method of obtaining a listing for shares which merely introduces existing shares on to the market rather than involving the issue of new shares. Where a company wishes its shares to be listed and it already has a wide range of shareholders, or is already listed on another exchange, such that the marketability of the shares on listing can be assumed, it is permitted to apply for a listing by means of introducing the shares to the market. In other circumstances, when the existing number of shareholders is too small for the marketability of the shares to be assumed, the company will be required to create a share issue to increase the number of shareholders.

Inventories (or stocks). Goods held by a firm which are available for sale to customers. The three categories of stock are raw materials, work-in-progress (WIP) and finished goods. Inventories are included as part of current assets in the firm's *Balance sheet* and form part of its *Working capital*.

Investment Company with Variable Capital (ICVC). A term used in regulatory contexts for an *Open-Ended Investment Company (OEIC)*. Authorisation as an ICVC is by compliance with *HM Treasury* ICVC Regulations, as well as further *FSA* regulations.

Investment firm. In the *MiFID* framework, a firm which provides or engages in 'core' investment services and activities, which include: receiving and transmitting orders; execution of orders on behalf of clients; dealing on own account; managing portfolios on a discretionary basis; investment advice; underwriting of financial instruments; placing of financial instruments; and operating a *Multilateral Trading Facility (MTF)*.

Investment grade. A term for *Bonds* that are a high level of credit quality: a bond rated BBB or above by Standard and Poor's and a bond rated Baa or above by Moody's. Any other bond is known as a *Junk bond* or *High yielding bond*.

Investment Management Association (IMA). An organisation representing the UK *Unit trust* and investment management industry, formed from the 2002 merger of AUTIF (Association of Unit Trusts and Investment Funds) merged with the FMA (Fund Managers' Association).

Investment manager. An *FSA*-authorised firm that manages designated investments in an account or portfolio under either a *Discretionary management* or non-discretionary management agreement.

Investment regulated scheme. A self-directed pension arrangement, where one or more members, or someone related to a member, directs, influences or advises on the investments which the scheme holds in relation to that member. A *Self-Invested Personal Pension (SIPP)* a type of investment regulated scheme.

Investment research. *MiFID* defines investment research as research or other information that is labelled or described as such or in similar terms, or is otherwise presented as objective or independent research (to use the FSA term). Under MiFID, other research material (what the FSA calls 'non-independent research') must be clearly identified as a 'marketing communication'.

Investment trust. A type of *Collective investment scheme*. An investment trust is a public limited company that issues shares to raise funds and then invests the funds in specified securities. When investors wish to realise their investment, they have to sell the shares to other investors in the secondary market or wait for the investment trust to be wound up. This feature gives the investment trust the description of being 'closed-ended'. Once the issue of shares has taken place, the size of the investment trust in terms of number of shares will not be changed. This is in contrast to *Unit trusts*, which are open-ended. See also *Open-Ended Investment Companies (OEICs)*.

Invisibles. In the context of a country's *Balance of payments*, see *Current account*.

Invoice amount. The amount paid by the buyer to the seller when a *Future* is delivered. The invoice amount is calculated by taking the reference price set by the exchange, known as the *Exchange Delivery Settlement Price (EDSP)*, and multiplying it by the number of contracts and the scaling factor, which converts the quotation into the price of one contract. Further adjustments may take place for certain futures, e.g. accrued interest on bond futures.

IOB. See *International Order Book*.

IOU. An abbreviation ('I Owe You') used for any debt instrument.

IPO. See *Initial Public Offer*.

IRR. See *Internal rate of return*.

ISA. See *Individual Savings Account*.

ISIN. An identifying number for a security in a widely adopted international system (International Securities Identifying Number) system. See also *CUSIP*.

ITBB. See *International Bulletin Board*.

J

Japan Securities Clearing Corporation (JSCC). A settlement agency for Japanese securities. All quoted shares in Japan are in registered form and bonds can be either bearer or registered. Securities cannot be held outside Japan and therefore local safe custody facilities are obligatory for non-residents wishing to deal in Japanese securities.

Jensen measure. A measure calculating the excess return that a portfolio generates over that predicted by the *Capital Asset Pricing Model* based on the *Beta* of the funds and is alternatively known as Jensen's Alpha.

Junk bond. A bond that is not of *Investment grade* – also known as a high yielding bond.

Kerb. A trading method on the *London Metal Exchange (LME)* when open outcry transactions may occur in all metal futures at the same time. Kerb trading takes place twice a day, at the end of both the first and second trading sessions. Each of the two trading sessions has two *Rings* that immediately precede the kerb trading.

Keyfacts documents. Initial disclosure documents to be supplied in respect of *Packaged products* business to a *Retail client* on first making contact. See *Menu* and *Initial Disclosure Document (IDD)*.

Know Your Customer (KYC). A self-explanatory principle underpinning all professional investment services. KYC helps firms in implementing procedures against *Money laundering*.

L

Laspeyre index. A base-weighted index, i.e. where all prices are weighted by the base date quantities.

Last trading day. The last day on which a *Derivatives* contract may be traded.

Lasting Power of Attorney. See *Power of Attorney*.

Layering. In *Money laundering*, the process of passing property through a complex series of transactions in order to conceal the owner or origin of the property. Other phases in the laundering of money are *Placement* and *Integration*.

LCH.Clearnet (LCH). A *Recognised Clearing House (RCH)*, formerly known as London Clearing House. Responsible for the clearing and settlement of derivative transactions effected on *LIFFE*, *LME* and *ICE Futures*, and also securities transactions on *virt-x*. LCH became the central counterparty to all *SETS* transactions in 2001.

Legal risk. The risk that contracts are not legally enforceable (*ultra vires,* meaning literally 'beyond the powers') or documented incorrectly, leading to a loss for the firm (see Box below).

Legal risk: examples

- In the late 1980s, the London Borough of Hammersmith and Fulham became extremely active in sterling swaps, suggesting speculation rather than hedging. The speculation was unsuccessful, and in 1991 the House of Lords ruled that the transactions were *ultra vires* – beyond the scope of the Borough's powers. Consequently, swap agreements between more than 130 councils and 75 major banks were rendered unenforceable *ultra vires*, and counterparties lost an estimated US$1 billion.

- Another example was the *ultra vires* claim in a lawsuit by Orange County, California against Merrill Lynch. Orange County's Treasurer had invested US$7.5 billion of the County's money in a risky, and eventually costly, portfolio of mostly interest-based securities. When US interest rates rose shortly thereafter, the Treasurer found himself in a liquidity trap and the County declared bankruptcy. Orange County claimed Merrill Lynch should have known that their contract violated several provisions of the California Constitution. There was a $400 million settlement in 1998.

Lender of last resort. A function of the *Bank of England,* as with other *Central banks,* indicating that the Bank is prepared, through the *Money markets,* to provide cash and liquidity. The Bank can do so by repurchasing bills.

BPP
LEARNING MEDIA

Less liquid (SEAQ securities). SEAQ stocks with a *Normal Market Size (NMS)* of 500 or less. Since these securities have less liquid trading than other SEAQ securities, details of trades done by *Market makers* in such stocks are not normally displayed on *SEAQ*. This enables the market maker to cover his position in the stock.

Letter of acceptance (or letter of allotment). A letter received by an investor who applies for shares on a new issue, where the application is successful. The letter provides evidence of the investor's ownership of the shares in the short term.

Letter of allotment. See *Letter of acceptance*.

Lender of last resort. The role of a *Central bank* in being ready to provide funds in exceptional circumstances. An example of its use, which is normally rare in the UK, was when the *Bank of England* provided a 'liquidity support facility' to the troubled bank Northern Rock during 2007.

Leverage. See *Gearing*.

Leveraged Buy Out (LBO). Takeover of a company, using borrowed funds. Typically, the assets of the company taken over are used as collateral. Sometimes called a Highly Leveraged Transaction (HLT).

Liabilities. Amounts owed by a firm to third parties other than shareholders. The third parties are effectively suppliers of finance to the company. Major examples include trade payables or *Creditors* (suppliers who sell goods to the company on credit) and bank loans and overdrafts.

LIBID. See *London Inter Bank Bid Rate*.

LIBOR. See *London Inter Bank Offered Rate*.

Life assurance (or life insurance). A form of insurance against an eventuality that is assured to arise, i.e. a person's death. There are various forms of life assurance policy, including: *Term assurance* policy, *Whole of life policy*, *Endowment policy*.

Life Assurance Premium Relief (LAPR). Tax relief given at 12.5% on premiums paid on qualifying life policies taken out before 14 March 1984.

Life insurance. See *Life assurance*.

Lifetime allowance. A limit on the total amount that can be accumulated under tax-advantaged pension arrangements for a single individual.

Lifetime mortgage. A generic term describing a range of secured lending products through which a home-owner may release equity tied up in their property.

LIFFE (*Euronext.liffe*). The London International Financial Futures and Options Exchange. A *Recognised Investment Exchange* and the main *Derivatives* exchange in the UK. LIFFE trades derivatives in equities, *Bonds*, interest rates, indices and commodities and is now part of Euronext.

LIFFE CONNECT®. The screen-based automated trading order book system for *Euronext.liffe* (LIFFE) products. LIFFE CONNECT® is an electronic trading platform that has been designed by LIFFE for trading its range of individual equity option contracts, replacing the former *Open outcry* method of trading for these products. Instead of traders meeting face to face in a pit on a trading floor, trading is conducted via computers located at the premises of LIFFE member firms and other market participants. Trading on LIFFE CONNECT® is conducted in an *Order-driven* rather than *Quote-driven* environment with buy and sell orders matched automatically in the virtual electronic market created between LIFFE and its market participants. The market operates anonymously with orders being matched on a strict price / time priority. Two-way prices, visible on the screen, represent firm buy and sell orders, instead of indicative quotes as existed in the open outcry market.

Light green fund. A *Fund* which applies an *SRI* or ethical investment approach, seeking less demanding levels of screening and corporate social performance, compared with the higher levels of screening used by *Dark green funds*.

LIMEAN. The *London Inter Bank Mean Rate*.

Limit order. An order specifying a limit at or below which a client agrees to buy, or at or above which a client agrees to sell.

Limited company. The most common type of company is limited by shares, but see also *Company limited by guarantee*. Companies limited by shares include 'LTD', 'Ltd', or 'Limited' in their title. Such companies are not allowed to issue their shares to the public. The liability of the shareholders is limited to the amount they agreed to pay for the shares. If the shares are 'fully paid' then there is no further liability. If they are *Partly paid shares*, then the shareholder will have to pay the remaining share price upon liquidation.

Limited liability. See *Limited company*.

Liquidator. The person responsible for winding-up a company, converting its assets into cash and distributing those assets to investors according to a legally defined priority, ending with ordinary shareholders.

Liquidity. The ease with which an investment may be realised in cash. Cash is the most liquid of all assets, since it can be used to buy any other asset. Investments traded on an *RIE* or *DIE* are considered to be more liquid than off-exchange traded products.

Liquidity risk. The risk of loss occurring through not being able to trade in a market or to obtain a price on a desired product when required.

Listed company. *Public limited companies* that are granted an official listing for their securities by the *UK Listing Authority* and are therefore permitted to have the shares traded in the secondary market under the rules of a *Recognised Investment Exchange*. Listed company status enables the company to raise substantial sums of money and enables investors to trade shares in the company easily. To achieve a listing, a company must comply with strict regulatory requirements designed to protect investors.

Listing agent. See *Sponsor*.

Listing Rules (LR). The rules of the *UK Listing Authority* to which companies must adhere in order to obtain and keep a listing on a *Recognised Investment Exchange*. The Listing Rules set out requirements for issuers. LR 9 Annex 1 contains the *Model Code for Directors Dealings*. The Listing Rules are designed to ensure that: there is a balance between providing issuers with ready access to the market and protecting investors; that applicants are suitable for listing; that securities are brought to market in an appropriate way that will ensure open and efficient trading; that there is full and timely disclosure of relevant information by listed companies; that there is confidence in the market; and that investors in a company have adequate opportunity to vote upon major changes in the company

Lloyd's of London. An insurance market, comprising (at 31 January 2006) 55 corporate members, 1,497 individual 'Names' with unlimited liability and 468 individual members with limited liability.

LME. See *London Metal Exchange*.

Local. Private trader operating on an exchange floor, whose activities help provide liquidity.

Location measure. A location measure attempts to indicate a central, long-run average value or return achieved. There are four location measures of importance: arithmetic mean, median, mode, and geometric mean.

London Clearing House. See *LCH.Clearnet (LCH)*.

London gold fix. The open fixing of a price for gold which takes place twice a day in London.

London Inter Bank Bid Rate (LIBID). The rate at which leading banks offer to take deposits on the *Money markets* from other leading banks.

London Inter Bank Mean Rate (LIMEAN). The average of *LIBOR* and *LIBID*.

London Inter Bank Offered Rate (LIBOR). The rate at which leading banks offer to make deposits on the *Money markets* with other leading banks. LIBOR is published by the *British Bankers Association* (BBA) after 11:00 am (and generally around 11:45 am) each day, London time, and is the mean of the eight middle values of inter-bank deposit rates offered by sixteen designated banks for maturities ranging from overnight to one year. LIBOR is a common rate of reference for sterling and other currencies, including the US dollar, the euro, the Japanese yen, the Canadian dollar, the Swiss franc, the Australian dollar, the New Zealand dollar, the Danish krona and the Swedish krona.

London Metal Exchange (LME). The UK *Derivatives* exchange that trades base metal *Futures* and *Options*, e.g. copper futures. LME is the largest world exchange for base metal derivatives. LME is a *Recognised Investment Exchange*. Trades are settled via *LCH.Clearnet* as the *Central counterparty*.

London silver fix. A similar process to the *London gold fix*. The silver fix takes place once a day.

London Stock Exchange (LSE). The principal London exchange for equity and bond trading. The LSE is a *Recognised Investment Exchange*.

Long position. Any position that has been purchased. For example, a long *Futures* position means that you have bought a future. A long call *Option* or a long put option means that you have bought the option, which gives you, the holder, the right to *Exercise* the option. Contrast with *Short position*.

Long hedge. A transaction that involves the purchase of a *Futures* contract in anticipation of actual purchases in the cash market. Such a transaction seeks to ensure that any increase in the cash price on the subsequent cash market purchase is offset by a profit on the futures position. Sometimes described as a consumer's hedge or as a price fix hedge.

Long run. In economics, the long run is a period sufficiently long to allow full flexibility in all inputs used.

Long straddle. See *Combination*.

Long-term Capital Management (LTCM). A highly leveraged hedge fund whose collapse in 2000 threatened financial markets.

Long-term currency swap. A contract that commits two counterparties to exchange, over an agreed period, two streams of interest payments in different currencies and, at the end of the period, to exchange the corresponding principal amounts at an exchange rate agreed at the start of the contract (there may or may not be an exchange of principal amounts at the start of the contract).

Longevity risk. The risk that liabilities to pay pensions will increase as pensioners live longer. It is difficult to meet this risk through investment in bonds. There is the possibility of a market for longevity risk developing through reinsurers, which could allow pension funds to lay off the risk, but such a market is not yet well established.

Lot. In relation to *Derivatives*, an alternative term for *Contract*.

LSE. See *London Stock Exchange*.

M0. One of the two official UK measures of money supply, the other being *M4*. M0 is referred to as the 'wide monetary base' or 'narrow money', also sometimes known as 'high-powered money'. M0 comprises notes and coins in circulation plus banks' operational deposits with the Bank of England.

M4. One of the two official UK measures of money supply, the other being *M0*.T M4 is referred to as 'broad money' or sometimes simply 'the money supply'. M4 comprises notes and coin in circulation with the public and non-bank firms *plus* private sector retail bank and *Building society* deposits plus private sector wholesale bank and building society deposits and *Certificates of Deposit*.

Macroeconomics. The study of the aggregated effects of the decisions of economic units. Concerned with issues such as unemployment and growth, macroeconomics looks at a complete national economy or the international economic system as a whole.

Maintenance margin. A type of *Margin* often applied in the US and sometimes in the UK. When a position is opened, *Initial margin* is called in the usual way and is credited to a maintenance margin account. However, *Variation margin* debits and credits are not payable/paid daily but are debited and credited directly against the maintenance margin account. When the balance in the account falls below a predetermined level (normally around two-thirds of the initial margin payment), the customer must fund the account back up to the initial margin level.

Malicious risk. The risk faced by all enterprises of malicious fraud, theft or intervention in a firm's systems by employees, disgruntled ex-employees, competitors and outsiders, including computer hackers and terrorists. Major incidents could cause a sudden complete shutdown of operations. Such a possibility has prompted companies to examine their disaster recovery procedures and to implement business continuity planning (BCP), business continuity management (BCM) or business availability management (BAM) solutions.

Manager of manager fund. A fund operated by placing money with a number of different managers.

Management buyout (MBO). Management buyouts are similar in all legal aspects to any other acquisition, with the main difference being that the buyers are managers of the business itself. As a result the seller (i.e. the company) is very unlikely to give anything but the most basic guarantees to the management (buyers), on the basis that they know a great deal about the company already. Often the motivation behind a MBO is an attempt to safeguard their own jobs, either because the business has been scheduled for closure or attempt to stop an outside purchaser bringing in its own management team. The management may also want to maximise the financial benefits they receive from the success they bring to the company by taking profits for themselves. MBOs are often used as a means of warding off aggressive buyers.

Mandatory offer. Under the *City Code on Takeovers and Mergers* (the Blue Book), when an investor either obtains control or consolidates control in a company that is covered by the Code, he must make a mandatory offer to buy out all the other shareholders. See also *Control* and *Consolidation of control*.

Mandatory Quote Period (MQP). The period during the day when a *Market maker* must make firm (i.e. guaranteed), two-way (i.e. buy and sell) prices in stocks in which they are registered. The period varies from market to market. For domestic *SEAQ*, it runs from 08:00 to 16:30.

Margin. A payment made by buyers and sellers of exchange-traded futures contracts and writers of exchange-traded options to demonstrate their ability to cover their potential losses on their position. The payment is made to the relevant clearing house. See also *Initial margin*, *Variation margin*, *Maintenance margin* and *Intraday margin*.

Marginal cost. The addition to total cost of producing one more unit of output.

Margin call. For a *Derivatives* position, a request for money by a clearing house to cover losses arising.

Market. A situation in which potential buyers and potential sellers (suppliers) of a good or service come together for the purpose of exchange.

Market abuse. A civil offence introduced by *FSMA 2000* to provide an alternative regime for prohibiting insider dealing and misleading statements. Market abuse is behaviour that will or would distort the market in the view of a *Regular market user*.

Market capitalisation. The total market value of a company's equity shares in issue: Share price × Number of shares.

Market economy. An economy in which decisions are generally made through the operation of the mechanism of prices.

Market If Touched (MIT). An order that becomes a *Market order* if a specified price is achieved. A buy MIT order is placed below the current market price; a sell MIT is placed above the current market price. Once the market hits the specified price, the order is then traded at the prevailing market price. An MIT order is generally used to open a position as opposed to closing one. It is in their relationship to the *Underlying* price that MIT orders differ from *Stop orders*.

Market failure. A situation occurring when a free market mechanism fails to produce the most efficient allocation of resources.

Market maker. A member of the Stock Exchange who has registered as such. There are Gr edged market makers (GEMMs) who are obliged to quote firm two-way prices (i.e. guarantee prices at which they will buy and sell) for all conventional *Gilts* or all index-linked gilts (I GEMMs) or both types of gilts. There are *Equities* or fixed interest market makers who are onl obliged to make firm two-way prices in stocks in which they are registered.

Market manipulation. Dishonestly or recklessly making a statement, promise or forecas that is misleading, false or deceptive, or dishonestly conceals material facts. Marke manipulation is an offence under s397 *FSMA 2000* if a person makes the statement, promis or forecast or conceals the facts for the purpose of inducing (or is reckless as to whether h may induce) another person to enter into an investment agreement. It does not matte

BPP)))
LEARNING MEDIA

whether the individual who entered into the investment agreement was the person to whom the statement was made: merely the act of making the statement is an offence.

Market-on-Close (MOC) order. A *Market order* that is submitted to execute as close as possible to the day's closing price.

Market operator. Under *MiFID*, a person who manages and/or operates a regulated market. The market operator may be the regulated market itself.

Market order. An order that is to be immediately executed at the best available price. On *SETS*, an 'at best' order entered during an auction call period which will have highest priority for matching.

Market portfolio. A portfolio that is representative of the whole stock market.

Market risk. See *Systematic risk*.

Market timing. A strategy of buying and selling securities in the hope of profiting from predicted market movements.

Market Value Reduction (MVR). A reduction which a life company may apply to surrendered *With profits* policies when market conditions are adverse, in order to protect those remaining in the with profits fund.

Markets in Financial Instruments Directive (MiFID). MiFID was adopted by the European Council in 2004 and is part of the *Financial Services Action Plan*. Its implementation date was 1 November 2007. MiFID has replaced the previous Investment Services Directive (ISD) and applies to all investment firms, e.g. investment and retail banks, brokers, assets managers, securities and futures firms, securities issuers and hedge funds. The aim of MiFID is to promote fair, efficient and integrated financial markets while facilitating competition between different trade execution venues. There were a number of reasons for revising the ISD. Under the ISD, *Passporting* firms had to follow local Conduct of Business rules, which affects the ease with which they could conduct cross-border activity. The ISD regime did not contemplate the use of *Multilateral Trading Facilities (MTFs)*. In the UK these are similar to what had previously been referred to as Alternative Trading Systems (ATSs) or Electronic Communication Networks (ECNs). Finally, the previous regime was outdated regarding core and non-core services and there was a lack of coverage of certain activities and financial instruments.

Marking to market. The process of valuing open positions, typically each evening at closing prices in order to determine that day's unrealised profit or loss. For example, marking to market is carried out daily by *LCH.Clearnet* in order to determine *Variation margin* payments to be made the next business day.

Matched bargain. See *Order-driven system*.

Matched trade. A trade in which the details recorded by buyer and seller are equal and opposite. Contrasts with an *Out trade*.

Matching concept. See *Accruals concept*.

Material interest. (1) A situation in which concerns over a firm's own position may cause *Conflict of interest* with the best interest of a customer. This conflict may be managed in a variety of ways including an *Independence policy*. In all cases, the interests of the customer must be placed above those of the firm. (2) A beneficial holding of three per cent or more of the shares of a public company. Under the Disclosure and Transparency Rules (DTR), where a person's holding of financial instruments in a company on the relevant market reaches or falls below three per cent of the voting rights, or increases or reduces across one full percentage point (e.g. 4.9% to 5.2%) then, they must notify the company within two business days (but four trading days for non-UK issuers).

MATIF. Marché à Terme International de France – the Paris *Futures* market, now a part of *Euronext* Paris.

Maturity. The final date on which the capital value of a bond is redeemed, i.e. the *Nominal value* (par) is repaid.

Maturity transformation. A feature of *Financial intermediation*, describing how *Financial intermediaries* accept deposits or investments of one term (typically short) while lending out funds over another term (typically the medium- or long-term).

Maximum publication level (MPL). Under *SEAQ*, defined as 6 × *Normal Market Size (NMS)*. Where a trade greater than this size is completed, it must be reported into SEAQ under the usual deadlines. However, display of trades in excess of the maximum publication level are usually delayed for 60 minutes. This gives the *Market maker* who has carried out the trade the opportunity to cover his position in the stock.

Memorandum of Association. A constitutional document of a company, detailing its name, its registered office, the fact that it has *Limited liability*, its trading objects and other relevant facts. See also *Articles of Association* – the other main constitutional document of a company.

Menu. A name given to the document entitled 'Key Facts: A Guide to the Cost of our Services' that is given to a retail client in a *Durable medium* by a firm carrying out *Packaged product* business on making initial contact or 'in good time' before the client is bound by an agreement to provide advice or the firm performs an act preparatory to providing advice. The Menu includes a section on the *FSA* and the purpose of the required menu, a section in which the firm gives details of 'Our services', the payment options offered (whether paying by fee or by commission/product charges), the typical fees or maximum commission the firm is likely to receive for a transaction, and an indication of the market average commission (for commission-based work). See also *Initial Disclosure Document (IDD)*.

Merit goods. Goods which are considered to be worth providing in greater volume than would be purchased in a free market, because higher consumption of the good is in the long term public interest. Education and health care are examples.

MFR. See *Minimum Funding Requirement*.

Microeconomics. The study of the reaction of households/individuals and firms to economic stimuli, and the effects upon demand and supply.

Mid-price. A page of *SETS* or *SEAQ* that gives the current mid-price between the best bid and offer prices of stocks. Where the colour of the price is blue, this indicates that the most recent price movement has been upwards. Where the colour of the price is red, this indicates that the most recent movement was downwards.

MiFID. The acronym for the *Markets in Financial Instruments Directive (MiFID)*.

MiFID business. Investment services and activities and, where relevant, *Ancillary services*, carried out by an investment firm to which MiFID applies.

Minimum Funding Requirement (MFR). The minimum funding requirement requires a *Defined benefit pension* fund's liabilities to be 100% funded. If the scheme falls below this level, the deficit must be remedied within ten years. In the case of falling below 90%, this must be remedied within three years.

Minimum Quote Size (MQS). The smallest quantity at which a *Market maker* is allowed to quote at for a *SEAQ* security, defined as 1 × *Normal Market Size (NMS)* of the stock.

Minority interests. Interests arising when a company has a subsidiary company in which it does not own all of the shares. The shareholders apart from the holding company are referred to as the minority interests. For example, where a holding company owns 80% of the shares in a subsidiary company, the remaining 20% of shareholders are the minority interests.

Misleading statements and practices. S397 *FMSA 2000* makes it a criminal offence to try to mislead the market or investors. Any person who dishonestly or recklessly makes a statement, promise or forecast that is misleading, false or deceptive, or dishonestly conceals any material facts is guilty of an offence if he makes the statement, promise or forecast or conceals the facts for the purpose of inducing (or is reckless as to whether he may induce) another person to enter into an investment agreement.

MIT. See *Market If Touched*.

Mixed economy. A type of economy where there is a combination of free markets and State intervention.

MOC order. See *Market-On-Close (MOC) order*.

Model Code for Directors' dealings. Part of the UKLA Listing Rules. A series of rules regulating when directors and relevant employees of listed and AIM companies are permitted to deal in the shares and related derivatives of the company of which they are employees. The purpose of the rules is to ensure that the public perceives that such directors and employees do not abuse their position in the company. The rules generally state that directors and relevant employees may not deal in the shares before a price-sensitive announcement or in a *Close period*. They also require *Clearance* from a designated director to deal. No trades should be undertaken in the *Close period* of 60 days before publication of the *Annual report* or, if shorter, the period from the end of the *Financial year* up to publication. The *Close period* before publication of the half-yearly report is from the end of the six-month period up to publication. For quarterly results, the *Close period* is one month prior to the announcement. If, as provided by the Disclosure Rules and Transparency Rules (DTR), *Interim Management Statements* are issued instead of quarterly reports, there is no *Close period* and companies must exercise discretion.

Modified duration. A measure linked to *Duration* which can be used to predict a change in price for a *Bond* given a change in interest rates. Defined as duration divided by (1 + *Gross redemption yield* of the bond).

MONEP. The Paris *Options* market. Now part of *Euronext* Paris.

Monetary policy. Government policy on the *Money supply*, the monetary system, *Intere rates*, *Exchange rates* and the availability of *Credit*.

Monetary Policy Committee (MPC). A committee of the *Bank of England* which sets official *Interest rates*. The MPC includes Bank of England representatives and industry expert

Money laundering. The process by which the sources of illegally obtained money disguised. The process is comprised of three phases: *Placement, Layering* and *Integration*. T *Proceeds of Crime Act 2002* identifies three offences that carry individual liability: assistir tipping off and failure to report a suspicion.

Money Laundering Reporting Officer (MLRO). The person within a firm who responsible for overseeing the firm's compliance with the systems and controls against *Mor laundering*.

Money market swap. An *Interest rate swap* generally with up to two years of life wh originally negotiated.

Money markets. The wholesale market for short-term money (usually less than one ye *Maturity*). Money can be put on deposit in the money markets for various maturities up to c year. Alternatively, short-term instruments such as *Treasury bills, Commercial bills a Certificates of Deposit* may be traded.

Money measurement concept. The concept is that, in accounting, every transaction item recorded is measured in monetary terms. If something cannot be recorded in mor terms, it is not recorded in the accounting books.

Money purchase pension scheme. See *Defined contribution pension scheme*.

Money supply. See *M0* and *M4*.

Money-weighted return. A measure calculated as the *Internal rate of return* of a *Fur* opening and closing values, along with any deposits into/withdrawals from the fund.

Monopolistic competition. A market structure in which the competing firms' products a close but not perfect substitutes for each other.

Monopoly. A market in which there is only one firm, the sole producer of a good which h no closely competing substitutes.

Moral hazard. The problem that someone who is insulated from *Risk* may behave differen from how they would behave if fully exposed to the risk.

Mortgage. A loan secured on real property (land and buildings).

Mortality release. In the context of annuities provided by a life company, which will p risks across all its annuitants, the release of funds arising from the fact that some annuita die earlier than others.

MPC. See *Monetary Policy Committee*.

MPL. See *Maximum publication level*.

MQP. See *Mandatory Quote Period*.

MQS. See *Minimum Quote Size*.

MTF. See *Multilateral Trading Facility*.

Mudaraba. In Islamic finance, an investment on someone's behalf by a more skilled person.

Mudarib. In a *Mudaraba* contract, an expert who manages the investment.

Multilateral Trading Facility (MTF). A system bringing together multiple buyers and sellers in financial instruments where firms provide services similar to those of exchanges by matching client orders. A firm taking proprietary positions with a client is not running an MTF. There has been much debate however surrounding the requirements to be imposed on MTFs. *MiFID* introduces the ability to *Passport* MTFs as a core service. The Committee of European Securities Regulators (CESR) has published standards they expect to be met by MTFs, including notifying the home State regulator of activities, fair and orderly trading, price transparency, clarity of systems and reduction of financial crime.

Multi-manager scheme. A type of investment scheme giving clients access to the products of a number of investment houses within a single unit-linked assurance-based or pension investment.

Multiplier. The ratio of the increase in national income to an initial increase in expenditure.

Multi-tied adviser. A financial adviser who has entered into agreements with two or more providers to sell the products offered or adopted by them.

Murabaha. In Islamic finance, a partnership contract for purchase and resale, allowing the customer to make purchases without taking out a loan and paying interest.

Musharaka. In Islamic finance, a partnership involving placing capital with another person and sharing in the risk and reward.

Mutual funds. A term for the US equivalent of *Collective investment schemes*.

Mutual guarantee. A type of guarantee operated by clearing houses where losses caused by a *Clearing member's* default are covered initially from the defaulting clearing member's assets (if any), and then from the guarantee fund contributed to by the clearing members. Only once this guarantee fund has been exhausted does the clearing house use its own resources to meet losses. No such fund exists with an *Independent guarantee*.

Mystery shopping. A tactic used by the *FSA* when it contacts firms posing as a retail consumer, to establish what a firm would say to a genuine customer.

Myners Review. In 2001, a review of institutional investment was undertaken by Paul Myners. The purpose of the review was to establish the extent to which institutions' approaches to investment decisions are rational, well informed, correctly incentivised, and undistorted.

N2. A name given to 30 November 2001, the date on which the *Financial Services and Markets Act 2000* came into force, replacing the Financial Services Act 1986.

Naked. A position in which the *Option writer* does not own the *Underlying asset* (*Call option* or does not have the cash to purchase the asset (*Put option*), i.e. he has an uncovered option position. Such a position involves effectively unlimited risks. Contrast with a *Covered* position where the risks are limited.

NAPF. See *National Association of Pension Funds*.

NASDAQ. The National Association of Securities Dealers Automated Quotation System: screen-based system for certain US shares, especially those of technology-related and growth enterprises. The NASDAQ is a *Recognised Overseas Investment Exchange* (*ROIE*).

NASDAQ Composite Index (often simply 'the NASDAQ'). A share price index covering all the 3,000 plus shares listed on the *NASDAQ* market. The NASDAQ is widely followed and quoted.

National Association of Pension Funds. A UK body providing representation and other services for those involved in designing, operating, advising and investing in pension schemes and other retirement provision.

National Futures Association (NFA). The US regulator responsible for the *Futures* markets.

National income. The sum of all incomes which arise as a result of economic activity, that from the production of goods and services.

National Savings and Investments (NS&I). Part of the UK Government's borrowing programme targeted towards retail investors. Products include *Savings Certificates* and *Premium Bonds*. As a Government agency, NS&I is exempted from the provisions of *FSM 2000*.

National Securities Clearing Corporation (NSCC). Part of the Depository Trust and Clearing Corporation (DTCC) group, the main function of the NSCC is to act as a checking and clearing service for dealer-traders and members of the exchange. It creates the underlying records on which transactions are settled and, where appropriate, generates book entry transfer via the DTCC. The net balance of money due from or to a broker is settled daily by single cheque with NSCC.

NCM. See *Non-clearing member*.

Negative equity. A situation where a home owner's *Mortgage* borrowings exceed the value of the property.

Net assets. In a company *Balance sheet*, Net assets *equals* Total assets *less* Total liabilities. Net assets will be equal to the *Shareholders' funds*.

Net assets per share (or net worth per share). An accounting ratio, defined as net assets divided by the number of shares in issue. The ratio enables comparison of the net assets per share with the share price. The share price will either be at a premium to net asset value or a discount.

Net debt/equity ratio. See *Gearing ratio*.

Net gearing ratio. See *Gearing ratio*.

Net pay arrangement. The scheme by which member contributions to an *Occupational pension scheme* and in-house *AVCs* are usually relieved for tax purposes, through *Pay As You Earn*, by deducting the contribution from pay before calculating the tax liability.

Net present value (NPV). The value, in present value terms, of a series of cash flows arising from a project, allowing for the cost of financing. An indicator of the value added to the firm by the project, the NPV method is the standard approach for financial project appraisal.

Net redemption yield. The *Gross redemption yield* on a bond less any tax charges suffered by the investor.

New York Mercantile Exchange (NYMEX). NYMEX is the largest exchange in the world for physical commodity futures. Its main divisions are the New York Mercantile Exchange and the New York Commodities Exchange (COMEX). NYMEX handles trading in energy, metals and other commodities which are bought and sold on the trading floor and through electronic trading computer systems. In early 2008, *CME Group* was discussing a deal to take over NYMEX.

Nikkei 225 Index. Once known as the Nikkei-Dow Index, this is a share price index covering the top 225 leading stocks traded on the Tokyo Stock Exchange. Like the *Dow Jones Industrial Average*, it is a price-weighted index. Movement in the share price of a small company may have as great an influence on the day's price movements as a comparable move in the price of a large one. With the Nikkei, this effect is heightened by the presence in the index of a number of traditional manufacturing firms, many of which are now considerably less important than they used to be. The Tokyo authorities have, for some time, attempted to encourage global markets to look at other, broader, more modern indices weighted according to market capitalisation, such as the TOPIX and the Nikkei 350, but global attention still tends to focus on the Nikkei 225.

Nil paid. See *Rights issue*.

NMS. See *Normal Market Size*.

Nominal value. The face value of a *Bond* or a share (which will not usually be the same as its price). Also known as par value. For a bond or redeemable share, it will usually indicate the value at which the bond or share will be redeemed by the issuer. The nominal value enables the interest payment on a bond to be calculated, being given by the nominal value of the holding multiplied by the quoted *Coupon* for the bond.

Nominated adviser (NOMAD). All companies on *AIM* are required to maintain a suitably qualified firm as their nominated adviser to assist them in complying with the rules and give assurance to investors. The nominated adviser will confirm in writing to the *UK Listing Authority* that the directors of the company have been advised and guided as to their responsibilities under the AIM rules and that the relevant rules have been complied with. A firm wishing to act as a nominated adviser must be on the register of nominated advisers held by the Stock Exchange and must be authorised under the *FSMA 2000*.

Nominee. A person or a firm such as a *Custodian* who holds securities on behalf of another. The nominee is the legal owner and it is their name that appears in the share register. The nominee has contractual obligations to the underlying beneficial owner.

Non-clearing member. Firms that are not clearing members of a clearing house, and do not therefore have the capacity to clear. Such firms must use the services of a general clearing member to have their trades cleared. They are typically smaller firms who do not meet the capital requirements set down by the clearing house.

Non-current assets (or fixed assets). Assets acquired for continued use within the business and not for resale. Sub-classified into: (1) intangibles including goodwill, (2) property, plant and equipment (PPE), and (3) investments such as interests in subsidiaries, associates, joint ventures and investments held for trade purposes.

Non-independent research. See *Investment research*.

Normal Market Size (NMS). Each listed company is allocated a NMS on the basis of the level of trading in the company's shares. The more active the trading, the higher the NMS. Obligations of *Market makers* and other parts of market regulation are set by reference to the NMS. See *Minimum quote size* and *Maximum publication level*.

Notice of Investigation. A formal Notice served by the *FSA* in the course of an investigation into the activities of a firm or approved person. Firms or individuals involved are normally served with a written Notice of Investigation unless the FSA believe the notice would prejudice their investigation.

Novation. The legal term that describes the conversion of a *Derivative* contract from being one simple bilateral contract between the original buyer and seller in the market into two contracts in which the clearing house becomes *Principal* to each, i.e. after novation, the clearing house is the counterparty (seller) to the buyer and separately the counterpart (buyer) to the seller.

NS&I. See *National Savings and Investments*.

NYMEX. See *New York Mercantile Exchange*.

NYSE. The New York Stock Exchange.

NYSE Euronext. The holding company created by the combination of NYSE Group Inc. and Euronext N.V. in 2007. NYSE Euronext, operating a large exchange group and offering diverse array of financial products and services brings together six cash equities exchanges five countries and six *Derivatives* exchanges.

Obligation Assimilable du Trésor (OAT). Long-term French Government debt.

Occupational pension scheme. A retirement benefits scheme set up by the employer for the benefit of the employees. Occupational (work-based) schemes tend to be *Defined benefit schemes*, although *Defined contribution schemes* are becoming increasingly common.

OECD. Organisation for Economic Co-operation and Development.

OEIC. See *Open-Ended Investment Company*.

Offer for sale. A method by which a company can issue shares to the public, having issued a *Prospectus*. Existing shareholders invite subscribers to purchase their shares.

Offer for subscription. An issue of shares by a company where investors are invited to subscribe for the shares directly with the company. A method of issuing shares when obtaining a listing for the first time on the Stock Exchange.

Offer price. The price at which a market maker is offering to sell shares. At any particular time, the offer price is almost always higher than the *Bid price* at which they will buy shares. For example, a quote of 510-515 indicates a bid price of 510 and an offer price of 515. The offer price is alternatively known as the *Asking price*.

Office of Fair Trading (OFT). The body responsible, *inter alia*, for investigating mergers and takeovers and recommending whether the merger should be investigated by the *Competition Commission*.

Official listing. See *Listed company*.

Offset. The extinguishing of a *Futures* or *Option* position by undertaking an opposite transaction. A sale offsets a long position and a purchase offsets a short position. Sometimes known as a closing trade.

Offshore centres. From a UK perspective, offshore centres are jurisdictions outside the UK. When an investment centre is offshore, it is not subject to UK tax or regulation, including investment protection rules. For example, investments located in offshore centres cannot lead to a claim on the *Financial Services Compensation Scheme (FSCS)* in the UK. Examples of commonly used offshore centres include the Isle of Man, the Channel Islands and Gibraltar.

OFT. See *Office of Fair Trading*.

Oligopoly. A market structure in which a few large suppliers dominate.

OMX. An equity index covering shares in Sweden.

OPEC. The Organisation for Petroleum Exporting Countries, an organisation to which many of the major oil producing countries belong.

Open positions. Market positions that have not been offset, i.e. are still capable of delivery.

Open-ended. The ability of a *Collective investment scheme* to issue an unlimited number of units. This is the case for *Unit trusts* and *OEICs*. In contrast, *Investment trusts* are closed-ended as they have a fixed number of issued shares.

Open-Ended Investment Company (OEIC). A form of *Collective investment scheme* that is designed to incorporate favourable aspects of both *Investment trusts* and *Unit trusts*. In legal terms, an OEIC is a company that issues shares, like an investment trust. However, whereas an investor in an investment trust who wishes to realise their investment has to sell their shares in the *Secondary market*, investors in an OEIC can sell the shares back to the company, as if it were a unit trust. OEICs can also be referred to as *Investment Companies with Variable Capital (ICVCs)*.

Open interest. The number of contracts left open in the market that are capable of delivery. With *Futures*, open interest is counted either by taking all of the long positions or all of the short. (To take both long and shorts would lead to double counting as they are different sides of the same contract.) With *Options*, all long calls and puts or all short calls and puts would be taken. Open interest gives a useful indicator as to the *Liquidity* in the market. High open interest figures suggest greater liquidity, as many who have open positions will wish to offset them before expiry of the contract.

Open market operations. The dealings of the *Bank of England* (or other *Central bank*) in the capital market. The Bank uses open market operations to control *Interest rates* and the volume of *Credit*.

Open offer. An issue of shares by a company for cash to existing shareholders on a basis that is *pro rata* to existing shareholdings. It is similar to a *Rights issue*, but with the key difference that the right to subscribe for shares in an open offer is not renounceable, i.e. it cannot be sold on to another investor.

Open outcry. A trading system in which members trade openly and verbally on a trading floor by 'crying' out their prices in a designated area normally known as a *Pit*. This form of trading is becoming increasingly rare as exchanges move to screen-based trading.

Open repo. A type of *Repo* in which the term (length) of the repo is not specified at the outset, in contrast to a *Term repo*. An open repo agreement can be terminated at any time by either party giving notice.

Opening auction. A period of ten minutes (plus possible extensions), starting at 07:50, which limit and market orders may be input into the *SETS* system. No automatic matching occurs until the end of the auction when the *Uncrossing algorithm* is run.

Opening order. An order type which requires that the order be filled during the official opening period in the market at the prevailing market price, not necessarily the opening price.

Opening purchase. A purchase transaction where rights or obligations are established. With an *Option* purchase, the buyer becomes the holder of the option.

Opening sale. A sale transaction where rights or obligations are established. With an *Option* sale, the seller becomes the *Writer* of the option.

BPP
LEARNING MEDIA

Operational risk. Defined by the Basel Risk Management Group as 'the risk of loss resulting from inadequate or failed internal processes, people and systems or from external events'. Operational risk may be broken down further into sub-categories such as *Reporting risk*, *Malicious risk*, *Legal risk* and *Regulatory risk*.

Opportunity cost. The cost of an item or course of action measured in terms of the alternatives forgone.

OPS. See *Occupational pension scheme*.

Option. A contract that gives the holder (the long) the right to buy or sell a specified asset at an agreed price on or before an agreed date in the *Future*. The right to buy an asset is a *Call option*. The right to sell is a *Put option*. Option contracts are sold by options *Writers*.

Order allocation policy. A firm's policy covering the fair allocation of aggregated orders, including how the volume and price of orders determines allocations, and the treatment of partial executions.

Order-driven system. A trading system where anyone wishing to buy or sell stock must take their order to the market and state at which price they are prepared to buy or sell the stock. Other market participants can then take the other side of the deal, creating a matched bargain. Contrasts with a *Quote-driven system*.

Order execution policy. The policy relating to firms' execution of client orders. Firms executing client orders must establish and implement an order execution policy, and it must monitor its effectiveness regularly. The policy must include, for each class of financial instruments, information on different execution venues used by the firm, and the factors affecting choice of execution venue. The firm should choose venues that enable it to obtain on a consistent basis the best possible result for execution of client orders. For each client order, the firm should apply its execution policy with a view to achieving the best possible result for the client. If orders may be executed outside a *Regulated market* or *Multilateral Trading Facility (MTF)*, this must be disclosed, and clients must give prior express consent. A firm must be able to demonstrate to clients, on request, that it has followed its execution policy.

Ordinary resolution. A shareholders' resolution to be voted on at the *Annual General Meeting* or *Extraordinary General Meeting* of a company, where a majority of votes cast at the meeting is needed for the resolution to be passed. See also *Special resolution*.

Ordinary shares. Also referred to as equities, equity shares or (in the US) as common stock. Shares that represent the right to participate in the residual assets of a business and which usually have voting rights. Shareholders will usually receive a *Dividend*, the level of which depends on how successful the company is. If the company is wound-up, the shareholders will be entitled to any assets left over only after all other persons with a claim have been paid off. Equity shareholders have limited liability, meaning that their liability to contribute money to the company, even if it is wound-up, is limited to the *Nominal value* of the share that they hold. If a share is fully paid as to its nominal value, then the holder of the share has no further liability in any circumstances.

OTC. See *Over-the-Counter*.

Out-of-the-money. A *Call option* or *Warrant* for which the *Exercise price* exceeds the price of the *Underlying asset* is out-of-the-money: it is not worth exercising as it has no *Intrinsic value*. For example, a call option on a share with an exercise price of 100p when the share price is 90p is out-of-the-money. A *Put option* is out of the money when the asset price exceeds the exercise price. For example, a put option on a share with an exercise price of

100p when the share price is 110p is out-of-the-money. See also *In-the-money* and *At-the-money*.

Out trade. A transaction for which the buyer and seller disagree over the exact details of the trade, i.e. it does not match. The disagreement may be over the number of contracts traded, or the price of the trade itself. Out trades should normally be resolved by the end of the business day on which they were traded. Contrast with *Matched trade*.

Overnight delivery risk. See *Herstatt risk*.

Over-the-Counter (OTC). Not traded on an exchange. The benefit of this is that the contract can be tailored to meet the investor's own particular requirements. In contrast, exchange-traded products are standardised but offer greater *Liquidity*. A major OTC market is the foreign exchange market, where banks trade directly with each other rather than through an exchange.

Overseas tax relief. Where an individual has an overseas source of income liable to UK tax on which he has already suffered overseas tax, he may be able to claim overseas tax relief reducing the amount of UK tax that is due on the income. The purpose of this is to prevent individuals suffering unfairly high or double rates of taxation, when both UK and overseas tax is taken into account.

Paasche Index. A current-weighted index, i.e. with all prices weighted by the current quantities.

Packaged product. A product which is one of the following: life policy, regulated *Collective investment scheme*, *Investment trust* savings scheme, *Stakeholder pension scheme* or *Personal pension plan* whether or not (in the case of the first three product types listed) it is held within a *PEP*, an *ISA* or a *Child Trust Fund (CTF)* and whether or not the packaged product is also a *Stakeholder product*.

PAL. Provisional Allotment Letter. See *Rights issue*.

Par value. See *Nominal value*.

Pari passu (for example, in relation to different issues of securities). Equal in all respects, without partiality.

Participating preference shares. See *Preference shares*.

Partly paid shares. Company shares on which the shareholder is still liable to pay an additional sum of money to the issuer when the outstanding amount is called by the directors. If the shareholder does not pay the outstanding amount, his share will be cancelled with no compensation. If the company is insolvent, the liquidator has the ability to sue shareholders for any unpaid amounts on partly paid shares.

Passive fund management. An approach to collective *Funds* whereby the fund manager does not attempt to outperform a selected *Benchmark*, unlike active fund management. Passive management generally involves seeking to follow a particular index. Passive fund management generally involves lower costs than active management. The passive approach has a theoretical underpinning deriving from modern portfolio theory and the *Efficient Markets Hypothesis*, in the idea that no mispriced securities exist if markets are working efficiently. See also *Full replication* and *Stratified sampling*.

Passporting. The concept of passporting allows a firm authorised in an *EEA* State to 'passport' that authorisation into another EEA State without having to participate in a full application for authorisation in that State. This makes it easier for firms to provide cross-border business. Thus, a firm may obtain authorisation in its home State, for example France, and then wish to open a branch or cross-border sell in a host State, for example the UK. Subject to the scope of the passporting Directives, the firm is not required to seek full authorisation from the UK regulator (the *FSA*). Their authorisation to conduct business in the UK jurisdiction will, instead, stem from the fact that the French regulator has already deemed the firm to be fit and proper. While opening a branch or cross-border selling is passportable, if the French firm wanted to set up an entirely separate UK entity, e.g. a separate UK subsidiary, this would not be passportable and the subsidiary would require full authorisation from the FSA.

PAYE. Pay As You Earn – a system whereby employees suffer income tax deduction at source from their salaries. Instead of paying the gross salary to the employee, the employer is obliged under law to deduct an appropriate amount of tax and remit this amount to *HMRC*.

Payment banks. *CREST participants* who guarantee payment for securities delivered to their client via *CREST*. Payment banks respond to instructions from members' (*Cash Memorandum Accounts (CMAs)*. All cash movements are effected outside CREST by debits/credits to their accounts at the *Bank of England*.

P/E ratio. See *Price-earnings ratio*.

Pension credit. A means-tested benefit designed to provide that pensioners receive at least a minimum level of income which is set by the government.

Pensions regulator. A regulatory body set up in 2005 to protect the interests of work-based (occupational or group personal pension) schemes and to promote good administration of the schemes it regulates.

PEP. See *Personal Equity Plan*.

***Per se* eligible counterparty**. A client automatically recognised as an *Eligible counterparty (ECP)* through being one of the following, including non-*EEA* equivalents: investment firms, credit institutions, insurance companies, UCITS *Collective investment schemes* and their management companies, pension funds and their management companies, other financial institutions authorised or regulated under the law of the EU or an EEA State, certain own-account *Commodity* derivatives dealers and 'local' derivatives firms, national governments, *Central banks* and supranational organisations.

***Per se* professional client**. See *Professional client*.

Perfect competition. A theoretical market structure in which no supplier has an advantage over another. It is assumed that there are an infinite number of buyers and sellers in the market place, that all consumers act rationally and all producers are profit maximisers, and that all producs are homogenous. All consumers and producers have perfect information and there are no barriers to entry or exit from the market.

Permanent Health Insurance (PHI). See *Income Protection Insurance*.

Permanent Interest Bearing Shares (PIBS). Irredeemable debt instruments issued by *Building societies*, usually paying a fixed rate of interest. When building societies have de-mutualised, turning themselves into banks, PIBS have become *Perpetual Subordinated Bond (PSBs)*.

Perpetual Subordinated Bonds (PSBs). See *Permanent Interest Bearing Shares (PIBS)*.

Perpetuity. An annual cash flow that will continue indefinitely.

Persistency. An indicator of the performance of financial advisers measuring the proportio of products sold that still remain in force (i.e. have not been cancelled by the customer) afte a specified period of time.

Personal Account Notice. Terms that form part of the employees' relevant contract o employment detailing the rules to be obeyed when employed by an *Authorised firm* but als when dealing for themselves.

Personal account dealing. Trading undertaken by the staff of a regulated business fo themselves. Such trades can create a *Conflict of interest* between staff and customers. A fir conducting *Designated investment business* from an establishment in the UK must establish, implement and maintain adequate arrangements aimed at preventing employees who are involved in activities where a conflict of interest could occur, or who has access to *Inside information*, from entering into a transaction which is prohibited under the Market Abuse Directive, or which involves misuse or improper disclosure of confidential information, or conflicts with an obligation of the firm to a customer under the regulatory system. The arrangements must also aim to prevent an employee, except in the course of his job, advising or procuring anyone else to enter into such a transaction, and disclosing any information or opinion to another person if the person disclosing it should know that, as a result, the other person would be likely to enter into such a transaction or advise or procure another to enter into such a transaction

Personal allowance. The first part of an individual's income, which is not liable to income tax.

Personal Equity Plan (PEP). A type of tax-free account to encourage investment in shares and *Bonds*, which preceded the *ISA*. No new PEPs could be opened after April 1999, but existing PEPs may continue and income and capital gains generated within the PEP are tax free.

Personal pension scheme. Defined contribution retirement schemes, set up by an individual who is, perhaps, self-employed or is not a member of an occupational scheme, are known as defined contribution pension schemes.

Phillips curve. A graphical illustration of the historic inverse relationship between the rate of wage inflation and the rate of unemployment.

PHLX. Philadelphia Stock Exchange.

Physical delivery. *Settlement* of a contract by the delivery or receipt of a financial instrument or commodity. This contrasts with *Cash settlement*, where no delivery of an *Underlying physical asset* takes place.

PIBS. See *Permanent Interest Bearing Shares*.

PIP. See *Primary Information Provider*.

Pit. The arena in which *Open outcry* trading in a particular product takes place. Each product or range of products will have its own designated *pit*. See also *Ring*.

Pit observer. An employee of an *Open outcry* exchange who is responsible for ensuring the orderly conduct of the market. Such an official will ensure compliance with the relevant regulations / trading rules, arbitrate in disputes, report trades and prices and, where applicable, trade public limit orders.

Placement. In *Money laundering*, the process of placing illicit proceeds with an institution or State which requires little or no disclosure concerning the ownership of those funds. Other phases in the laundering of money are *Layering* and *Integration*.

Placing. An issue of shares where the issuing house places the shares directly with its client base rather than inviting applications for the shares from outside third parties – also known as *Selective marketing*. A method of issuing shares where a company is obtaining a listing for the first time, this method of issuing securities is also common in *Bond* markets.

PLUS Markets. PLUS Markets plc (PLUS) is a *Quote-driven* (*Market-maker*) electronic trading platform currently trading a range of securities including full coverage of all London-listed shares, such as the *FTSE 100*, and unlisted shares quoted on the *AIM* and PLUS markets. It is a *Recognised Investment Exchange* in the UK and a *Market operator* under *MiFID*, authorised to operate both *Secondary* and *Primary markets*. The PLUS trading platform (known as the 'secondary market' in equity markets terminology) offers an execution venue for trading securities listed elsewhere in London and Europe, as well as its own PLUS primary market, combining independent price formation with trade reporting. PLUS has replaced the former 'Ofex'.

Policy of independence. See *Independence policy*.

Position. A long or short market commitment, an obligation, or right, to make or take delivery.

Position limit. A limit set by an exchange that restricts the number of contracts a person or group of connected persons may hold in a particular product. Position limits are put in place to ensure that entities cannot establish a dominant and potentially destabilising position in a product (sometimes known as a 'squeeze' or 'cornering the market'). Position limits are common on many US exchanges, but not on UK exchanges.

Potentially Exempt Transfer (PET). When an individual makes a gift to another person, the gift will usually be liable to *Inheritance tax* only if the donor dies within seven years of making the gift. If the donor survives for seven years, the gift will be exempt from inheritance tax. At the date the gift is made, its final status is therefore uncertain and it is referred to as a *Potentially Exempt Transfer*.

Pound cost averaging. If equal regular (e.g. monthly) investments are made, for example in a *Unit trust* or *OEIC*, then relatively fewer units will be purchased when the price is relatively high. More units will be purchased when the price is relatively low. This effect is known as pound cost averaging.

Power of attorney. A document made by a person (the 'donor') which appoints another person (the 'attorney' or the 'donee') or persons to act on the donor's behalf, for example in signing documents. A power of attorney is thus the written appointment of an agent and could be used, for example, when a person goes abroad for a long time. A Lasting Power of Attorney under the Mental Capacity Act 2005 (formerly called an Enduring Power of Attorney) can be used by an elderly person who is mentally capable of making decisions in preparation for a time when he may be incapable of making decisions.

PPS. See *Protected Payment System*.

Pre-emption rights. When a UK company issues new shares, it is obliged by law to give existing shareholders the opportunity to purchase the new shares on a basis *pro rata* to their existing shareholding in the company. This right is usually implemented by means of a *Right issue*. Pre-emption rights may be disapplied where a shareholders' resolution to that effect has been passed.

Preference shares. Shares in a company which usually receive a fixed *Dividend* each year and which, if redeemed, are redeemed at *Par value*. Although the dividend is fixed, it is not guaranteed. However, if the company fails to pay ('passes') the preference dividend, it will not be allowed to pay an ordinary dividend for the year to ordinary shareholders. Where the preference shares are cumulative, any arrears of preference dividend will also have to be paid prior to the ordinary dividend being paid in any year. Preference shares may be redeemable, in which case they will be redeemed at a set date. They may also be convertible. Finally, they may be participating, which means that, in addition to the fixed dividend, they will receive a variable dividend dependent on the performance of the company. Contrast with *Ordinary shares*.

Preferred stock. An alternative term for *Preference shares*.

Premium. (1) When a *Bond* is redeemed at a premium to par, this means that the redemption value exceeds the nominal value of the bond. (2) When a currency is trading at a premium in the forward *FX* market, this indicates that it is strengthening in the forward market relative to the spot market. A forward premium is deducted from the spot quote to give the forward quote. (3) The price paid to acquire an *Option*. (4) The amount by which a *Futures* price exceeds its *Fair value*.

Premium Bonds. A form of government borrowing organised by the government agency *National Savings & Investments*. Investors buy serially numbered premium bonds at a cost of £1 each. Each month a random draw is made of numbers for a range of prizes. The total value of the prize fund is calculated by reference to a percentage of the total value of bonds outstanding. An investor may redeem bonds at par value at any time. Winnings are tax free. Premium bonds are not specified investments as they are not tradeable.

Premium put. The right of an investor to redeem a *Bond* for cash at a *Premium* to nominal value.

Prepayment. Where money has been paid by an entity for a service not yet received. For example, rent might be paid in advance. The prepayment – effectively, the value of the service yet to be provided – is treated as an asset on the *Balance sheet*.

Prescribed market. Markets that are covered by the *Market abuse* offence. This covers all UK *RIEs*, as well as *PLUS Markets*.

Present value. The value of a series of future cash flows, adjusted to their present value using an appropriate discount rate.

Preventive controls. *Internal controls* that are designed to prevent errors occurring. Preventive controls attempt to tackle the root causes of risk and are most effective when incorporated within processes at the outset by anticipating a risky outcome. A key preventive control is the *Segregation of duties*. Contrast with *Detective controls*.

Price-driven system. See *Quote-driven system*.

Price-earnings ratio (P/E ratio). An accounting ratio defined as the share price divided by the earnings per share. Broadly speaking, the higher a company's P/E ratio, the more expensive the company and the more highly rated it is.

Price factor. The figure used to convert the price of a bond future into the price of a deliverable *Bond*. This is done to bring all deliverable bonds on to a common basis. Sellers will receive more for a higher *Coupon* (more expensive) bond than for a lower coupon (cheaper) bond.

Price fix hedge. See *Long hedge*.

Price limit. A limit set by an exchange which restricts the amount by which a product's price may vary in a trading day, in an attempt to prevent prices moving too far or too fast within a trading session. If the limit is breached during the session, trading is halted for a set period of time, the theory being that this reduces any panic amongst traders and calms the market. At the end of the trading halt, trading resumes. Few UK exchanges impose price limits, as they prevent investors from trading when they wish, and can therefore have potentially serious consequences.

Price Stabilising Rules. Stabilisation is an allowable type of price support undertaken for certain new issues of securities. The rules, set out in MAR 2 in the *FSA Handbook*, give effect to the EU Buy-Back and Stabilisation Regulations. The rules allow a stabilising manager (usually the authorised firm leading the issue) to buy in the market to alleviate downward sales pressure caused by short-term investors, thus maintaining the share price at or near the offer price. There may only be one stabilising manager. Stabilisation generally may last for no more than 60 days after the allotment of securities and details must be notified to the market. As stabilisation is a form of price distortion there are specific defences for the stabilising manager to some of the *Market abuse* offences set out in s118 and the criminal offences under s397 *FSMA 2000* and the *Criminal Justice Act 1993*.

Primary dealer. The US name for *Gilt-edged market makers*.

Primary Information Provider (PIP). An officially recognised provider of price-sensitive market news. Companies can make price-sensitive announcements under their *Continuing obligations* to the *Listing Rules* through one of five information services approved by the *UK Listing Authority*. See also *Regulatory Information Service*.

Primary market. The market for the initial issue of securities by an issuer to investors, to be distinguished from the *Secondary market*, where investors trade the security among themselves.

Principal. A market participant who is acting for their own account when buying and selling as opposed to acting as *Agent* for another person.

Principal Private Residence. An individual's main home, which is generally exempt from capital gains tax on disposal.

Principles for Businesses. Eleven principles that all *FSA*-authorised firms must adhere when they are performing regulated activities.

Principles for Businesses

1   **Integrity**. A firm must conduct its business with integrity.

2   **Skill, care and diligence**. A firm must conduct its business with due skill, care and diligence.

3   **Management and control**. A firm must take reasonable care to organise and control its affairs responsibly and effectively, with adequate risk management systems.

4   **Financial prudence**. A firm must maintain adequate financial resources.

5   **Market conduct**. A firm must observe proper standards of market conduct.

6   **Customers' interests**. A firm must pay due regard to the interests of its customers and treat them fairly.

7   **Communications with clients**. For customers – A firm must pay due regard to the information needs and communicate information to them in a way that is clear, fair and not misleading. For eligible counterparties – A firm must communicate information in a way that is not misleading.

8   **Conflicts of interest**. A firm must manage conflicts of interest fairly, both between itself and its customers and between a customer and another client.

9   **Customers: relationships of trust**. A firm must take reasonable care to ensure the suitability of its advice and discretionary decisions for any customer who is entitled to rely upon its judgement.

10   **Clients' assets**. A firm must arrange adequate protection for clients' assets when it is responsible   for those assets.

11   **Relations with regulators**. A firm must deal with its regulators in an open and co-operative way and must disclose to the FSA appropriately anything relating to the firm of which the FSA would reasonably expect notice.

Priority. This determines the order in which a member's transactions will be settled within *CREST* once the intended settlement date has been reached. Priorities are either automatically assigned or selected by the member. Priorities range from 0-99 with higher priority transactions, e.g. 90 settling before lower priorities, e.g. 50.

Private equity. Investment in a company through a negotiated process. The involvement in the company is typically one of transformational active management. Private equity is a major source of funds for: venture capital start-ups; private medium-sized firms seeking expansion finance; public firms seeking finance for a *Management buy out* or a *Leveraged buy out*; and firms in financial distress (or 'special situations'). The private equity firm will generally receive a return through an *Initial Public Offering (IPO)*, a sale or merger of the controlled company, or a recapitalisation. The size of the private equity market has increased substantially, and nearly US$135 billion was invested globally in 2006.

Private limited company. A company with limited liability (Limited or Ltd) which is not permitted to issue shares to the public. This contrasts with a *Public limited company (plc)*.

Private person. An individual not performing a *Regulated activity* (e.g. the private client of a broker) who has the right of action under s150 of *FSMA 2000* to sue for damages as a result of a contravention of certain rules by an authorised firm. This right exists in addition to common law actions such as negligence or misrepresentation. However, s150 provides a privileged right of action as there is no need to prove negligence – it is simply enough that there has been a rule breach leading to loss. Note that the *FSA Principles for Businesses* and *Statements of Principle for Approved Persons* are not deemed to be rules for the purposes of this right. A private person can also include businesses in very limited circumstances. For example, a company setting up an occupational pension scheme for its employees would be treated as a private person. Additionally, s71 *FSMA 2000* allows a private person to seek damages or compensation from an authorised person where they have suffered loss due to the fact that they have dealt with an unapproved individual, such as where the private person has lost out as a result of advice obtained from an unapproved investment adviser.

Privatisation. The transfer by government of State-run activities to the private sector.

Probate value. The agreed value of an individual's estate at death.

Proceeds of Crime Act 2002. Legislation that contains *Anti-money laundering* provisions.

Producer's hedge. See *Short hedge*.

Product differentiation. Differences among products giving some market power by acting as a barrier to entry.

Production possibility frontier. The range of possibilities from employing the resources of the economy.

Productivity. The relationship between the output of goods and services and the inputs of resources used to produce the goods and services: a measure of the efficiency with which output has been produced.

Professional client. A category of client enjoying less regulatory protection than a *Retail client*. *Per se* professional clients are undertakings meeting certain size and other conditions which serve to classify them as professional, although such clients may be re-categorised as *Retail clients*. Retail clients may opt up to be treated as professional clients and such clients are referred to as 'elective' professional clients. Although broadly similar to an 'expert' private customer under pre-MiFID Conduct of Business rules, the qualifying criteria for a retail client to become an 'elective' professional client are more detailed under *MiFID*.

Profit. A measure of total revenue minus total cost of any level of output. In economic theory, the residual return of the entrepreneur.

Profit and loss account. (1) A statement showing a company's income and expenditure over a period of time, usually one year. In international *GAAP* terminology, the term *Income statement* is used. (2) A reserve in a company's *Balance sheet*, representing the accumulated profits that a company has generated since its incorporation. This reserve is distributable with regard to *Dividend* distributions.

BPP
LEARNING MEDIA

Prohibition Order. An Order under s56 *FSMA 2000*, which allows the *FSA* to prohibit individuals from carrying out specified functions in relation to *Regulated activities* within the investment industry. A Prohibition Order may be issued in respect of anyone, whether or not they are an approved person.

Project Turquoise. An initiative backed by seven of the *LSE's* largest customers, and the Depository Trust & Clearing Corporation (DTCC). The founding group of banks – Goldman Sachs, Citigroup, Merrill Lynch, Morgan Stanley, UBS, Deutsche Bank and Credit Suisse – aims to create a user-owned Pan-European exchange offering lower trading costs. Project Turquoise is an example of a *Multilateral Trading Facility (MTF)*. MTFs are encouraged under *MiFID*. Originally planned for launch when MiFID took effect on 1 November 2007, Project Turquoise has been delayed beyond this date. Talks about a merger with *PLUS Markets* ended in October 2007. The Turquoise consortium expects that the system will be able to provide dealing services at a 50 per cent discount to traditional exchanges. The project, based in London, is a hybrid system allowing trading both on and off traditional exchanges.

Prompt date. The term used on the *LME* to describe a *Future's* delivery day. LME contracts have daily prompt dates for all business days out to three months, then at less frequent intervals out to 27 months.

Property. The asset class comprising interests in land and buildings, also known as real estate.

Prospectus. A document prepared by a company that is issuing securities to the public.

Protected claim. This means certain types of claims in respect of deposits and investment business. Protected investment business means *Designated investment business*, the activities of the manager / trustee of an authorised *Unit trust* and the activities of the authorised corporate director / depository of an ICVC. These activities must be carried on either from an establishment in the UK or in an *EEA State* by a UK firm who is *Passporting* their services there.

Protected Payment System (PPS). The automated payments system operated by *LCH.Clearnet* for the collection and payment of *Margin*. LCH.Clearnet has a mandate over its *Clearing members'* bank accounts, and can therefore pass instructions for margin monies (*Variation margin* debits and *Initial margin*) to be electronically transferred from the clearing members' accounts to its own account to cover margin calls. In addition, it can electronically credit the clearing members' bank accounts with variation margin credits and the return of initial margin.

Protected rights. Rights arising from contracted-out contributions to a *Money Purchase Pension Scheme*.

Protection. The practice of shielding sectors of the economy from foreign competition, for example through tariffs or import quotas.

Provisional Allotment Letter (PAL). See *Rights issue*.

Provisions. Liabilities where the company is uncertain as to the amount or timing of the expected future costs. For example, if a company is subject to a lawsuit, it may provide now for the expected liability on loss of the lawsuit. This is an example of applying the *Prudence concept*.

Proxy voting. The exercise of voting rights through a third party, based on a legally valid authorisation and in conformity with the investor's instructions. Depending on the country in which the 'proxy' is being exercised, the third party might be a bank, a person designated by the company, another shareholder or the chairman of the shareholders' meeting.

Prudence concept. One of the fundamental *Accounting concepts*. Accounts must be prepared on a prudent basis. This implies that revenue must never be shown in the accounts until the cash realisation of the revenue is reasonably certain. On the other hand, costs arising as a result of past actions should be provided for immediately, even if the cash will not be paid over until the future.

Prudential regulation. The overall aim of prudential rules is to ensure that firms remain solvent by having greater assets at their command than they will need to cover their positions. This is often referred to as *Capital adequacy*, financial resources or prudential regulation. An assessment of capital adequacy is arrived at by comparing the actual resources of the business (its financial resources) against the overall requirement that it may have to finance (it financial resources requirement). The firm's financial resources requirement is arrived at b placing a figure on various risks such as credit risk, market risk and foreign exchange risk.

PSNCR. See *Public Sector Net Cash Requirement*.

PTM levy. A charge of £1, payable by both the buyer and seller in a share transaction of ove £10,000 to fund the work of the Panel on Takeovers and Mergers (*Takeover panel*).

Public goods. Goods whose production is organised by the government, such as defence ar policing.

Public Interest Disclosure Act 1998. Legislation covering *Whistleblowing* procedures th apply to authorised firms.

Public limited company (PLC or plc). A company which, by registering as a plc and adheri to the resulting legal requirements, has the ability to issue shares to the public. In contrast, *Private limited company* is not permitted to issue shares to the public. Only some plcs becor *Listed companies*.

Public sector net cash requirement (PSNCR). The annual excess of spending ov income for the entire public sector.

Purchase fund. A way of redeeming *Bonds* in instalments over the life of the bond, by mea of bonds being repurchased prior to final *Maturity* in the market at the current market pric See also *Sinking fund* and *Bullet form*.

Purchasing power parity (PPP) theory. An explanation of currency exchange rates wh holds that, over the long-run, exchange rates will tend towards the rates that equate purchasing power of equivalent amounts of the different currencies.

Put/call parity. The relationship between *Option* and *Futures* prices. The prices of options and futures on the same underlying product must be linked because it is possible synthetically to create futures positions with the use of options. Otherwise, *Arbitrage* would be possible. For options on futures, the sum of the *Call option* and *Put option* prices must be equal to the futures price less the *Exercise price* of the option. For options on physicals, this formula is amended slightly so that the exercise price of the options is discounted back to today's values.

Put option. A contract that confers upon the holder the right, but not the obligation, to sell an asset at a given price on or before a given date.

Put warrant. See *Covered warrant*.

Qualified Investor Scheme (QIS). A regulatory term for *Collective investment schemes* open to institutions and expert private investors, with fewer consumer protection rules that apply to retail schemes.

Qualifying Corporate Bond (QCB). A bond that is non-convertible and denominated in *Sterling*. QCBs comprise all company loan stock and *Debentures* (except loan stock convertible into shares) that are issued in sterling and bought by the investor after 13 March 1984, and *Permanent Interest Bearing Shares (PIBS)*, which are issued by *Building societies*. QCBs are exempt from capital gains tax.

Quantity theory of money. A theory which holds that changes in the level of prices are caused predominantly by changes in the supply of money.

Quanto swap. See *Diff swap*.

Qard. In Islamic finance, a loan free of profit, such as a bank current account.

Quick ratio. See *Acid test ratio*.

Quorum. The minimum number of members (two) of a company required to be present for a meeting to be legally effective under the Companies Act 1985.

Quote-driven system. A system whereby market makers provide quotes at which people can trade in stocks. Also known as a price-driven system. Contrasts with an *Order-driven system*.

Random walk hypothesis. A theory suggesting that future share price movements cannot be predicted from details of historical movements.

Range. The difference between the highest and lowest observed values in a set of data.

Ratio analysis. The calculation of performance indicators, such as those set out in the 'pyramid' below, from the financial information available on a company.

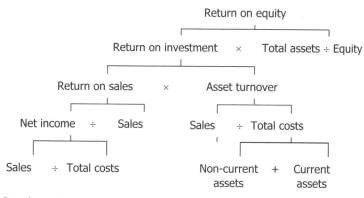

RDC. See *Regulatory Decisions Committee*.

Real estate. See *Property*.

Real rate of return. The rate of return after adjusting for price *Inflation*.

Real Time Gross Settlement (RTGS). A system ensuring payment instructions are transmitted on a transaction-by-transaction basis between direct members of the system and are settled individually across central bank accounts in real time. Any intra-day central bank credit given to participating banks is fully collateralised in order to eliminate settlement risk.

Receivables (or debtors). Amounts owed to a firm. Accounts receivable record the amounts owed. Amounts owed by customers are known as trade receivables (trade debtors).

Recognised Clearing House (RCH). An organisation that provides clearing services for one or more markets. Only RCHs are able to operate as clearing houses in the UK. Recognition is granted by the *FSA* to those clearing houses meeting its requirements. Currently *Euroclear UK & Ireland* and *LCH.Clearnet* are RCHs.

Recognised Investment Exchange (RIE). An organisation, based in the UK, providing a market place in investments and recognised by the *FSA*. While the exchanges must be licensed or 'recognised', they are exempt from authorisation.

Recognised Overseas Investment Exchange (ROIE). An exchange established outside the UK, yet able to act as an exchange within the UK often with a screen-trading system. Examples include the *NASDAQ*. No separate distinction is made between a *RIE* or a ROIE under *FSMA*: ROIEs as well as RIEs are exempt from *FSA* authorisation.

Reconciliation. A process of proving that a firm's books or records are accurate. For example, each major component of a company's securities and cash positions must be reconciled in its own right. These will cover trading positions, cash accounts, stock deposit positions, margin accounts (where applicable) and collateral accounts. Checks will be carried out to ensure first that the firm's records agree internally, and second that the records agree with external sources such as *Counterparties*, *Custodians* and clearing houses.

Record date. In relation to corporate actions, including *Dividend* payments, those investors whose names appear on the register as at the record date (also called the 'books closed date' will receive the benefit from the company. The sequence of *Cum dividend* period, *Ex-dividend* period and record date are illustrated below.

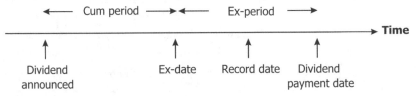

Record keeping. Under *MiFID*, firms must keep relevant data relating to all transactions financial instruments which they have carried out whether on their own account or on behalf of a client for at least five years. Other time limits may apply to non-MiFID business.

Reduction in yield. The amount by which investment yield on an investment is reduced, percentage terms, by charges.

Reference scheme. A broad quality test of the benefits that a *Defined Benefit Pension Scheme* must provide in order to be Contracted Out of the *State Second Pension* scheme.

Register Update Request (RUR). A *CREST* instruction sent to a company *Registrar* requesting that the register is amended to reflect a trade conducted. The registrar must register or reject within two hours of receiving this request. The registrar must be able distinguish between CREST holdings (dematerialised) and non-CREST holdings (paper certificates).

Registered pension scheme. A retirement benefits scheme that is registered with *HMRC* and, as a result, enjoys the usual tax advantages associated with pension arrangements.

Registered securities. Shares or bonds whose ownership is recorded in a central register, opposed to *Bearer securities*.

Registrar. The department or organisation appointed by a company responsible for upkeep of a legal record (the register) of the company's shareholders.

Regular market user. A regular user is defined in s118 *FSMA 2000* as a reasonable person who regularly deals on that market in investments of the kind in question. The offence of *Market abuse* uses this hypothetical person to test for inappropriate behaviour.

Regulated activity. An activity set out in the Regulated Activities Order (as amended), such as dealing in or managing investments, which requires authorisation under *FSMA 2000*.

Regulated collective investment scheme. An *Investment Company with Variable Capital (ICVC)*, an authorised *Unit trust* (AUT) or a recognised *EEA* or other overseas scheme that meets certain criteria enabling it to be freely marketed to private customers.

Regulated market. A multilateral system operated and/or managed by a *Market operator*, which brings together or facilitates the bringing together of multiple third-party buying and selling interests in financial instruments – in the system and in accordance with its non-discretionary rules – in a way that results in a contract, in respect of the financial instruments admitted to trading under its rules and/or systems, and which is authorised and functions regularly and in accordance with *MiFID*. This includes regulated *EEA* exchanges.

Regulatory Decisions Committee. A body separate from the *FSA* who will look at a disciplinary case and decide whether or not to take action. The RDC is appointed by the FSA board and is therefore answerable to the FSA board for its decisions, but deliberately set up outside of the FSA's management structure so that it can make decisions independently. Only the chairman of the RDC is a FSA employee. The rest of the RDC's membership is drawn from current or recently retired practitioners within financial services and other suitable individuals representing public interest. The RDC can meet as a committee or in panels, the size of which will depend on the nature of the case under investigation.

Regulatory Information Service (RIS). A body to whom disclosures are made in order to comply with the UK *Listing Authority* rules on disclosure, one example of which is the *Regulatory News Service*. See also *Primary Information Provider*.

Regulatory News Service (RNS). Part of the Stock Exchange system for ensuring announcements by *Listed companies* are disseminated fairly through the market. It is also one of the *Regulatory Information Services* and is known as a *Primary Information Provider (PIP)*.

Regulatory risk. The risk that a firm breaches regulators' rules or codes of conduct

Renounceable document. A document for which legal title can be transferred to another person.

Repo. See *Repurchase agreement*.

Reporting risk (or information risk). The risk that the reports and sources of information that management use to make their decisions contain incorrect or misleading information. Incorrect and misleading information can lead management to make wrong policy decisions and to make corrective action in the wrong direction. Misleading, distorted or delayed information can lead to trends or mistakes not being identified and, thus, ignored.

Repurchase agreement (sale and repurchase agreement, or repo). An agreement to sell a *Bond* (often a government bond) at one price, with a simultaneous agreement to repurchase the bond at a later date, at a price agreed today. Effectively, a repo trade enables the holder of a bond to borrow money while using the bond as financial collateral with the lender. The lender has done a reverse repo.

Reserves. Part of *Shareholders' funds* on a company's *Balance sheet*. All parts of shareholders' funds apart from *Share capital* are reserves, such as the *Share premium account* reserve, the *Profit and loss account reserve* and the *Revaluation reserve*.

Residence. In tax law, an individual is considered to be resident in the UK in a *Fiscal year* he remains in the UK for 183 days or more in the fiscal year in question or if in the past four fiscal years he has stayed in the country for an average of 92 days or more per year. Anyone who is resident in the UK is liable to pay income tax on their worldwide income, subject to certain exceptions. In addition, they are liable to pay capital gains tax on any capital gains that they make worldwide. Individuals who are not UK residents are usually only liable to pay income tax on their income from UK sources.

Residual settlement. *Settlement* outside *CREST* whereby, if the counterparties are *CREST members*, CREST permits the use of the *CCSS* and CREST payment instructions.

Restitution Order. An instruction to make good any losses and to place the investor in a similar financial position prior to any wrongdoing. Under *FSMA 2000*, the *FSA* has the power to order restitution directly and to apply to the High Court for a Restitution Order.

Retail client. A client who is not a *Professional client* nor an *Eligible counterparty (ECP)*. Either on its own initiative or following a client request or written agreement, a *per se Eligible counterparty* may be re-categorised as a professional client or retail client, and a *per se professional client* may be re-categorised as a retail client. Such re-categorisation will enable the client to gain a higher level of regulatory protection.

Retail Prices Index (RPI). A measure of the rate of inflation in the UK, the RPI calculates the cost of buying a standard basket of goods and expresses this as a percentage of the base year index. For example, when the base year is 100 and the current retail price index is 150, this indicates that prices have risen by 50% since the base year. Note, however, the constituents of the basket change over time to reflect changing consumer preferences.

Return on capital employed (ROCE). An accounting ratio designed to assess the underlying profitability of a company. ROCE is defined as profits before interest and tax divided by capital employed, and is expressed as a percentage. The capital employed comprises *Shareholders' funds plus Creditors* due after more than one year *plus* any long-term provisions for *Liabilities* and charges, Broadly speaking, the higher the return on capital employed, the more successful the company.

Revaluation reserve. Part of *Shareholders' funds*, this type of reserve arises when an asset is revalued in a company's *Balance sheet*. The profit on revaluation is considered to be part of shareholders' funds but is shown in a separate reserve to highlight the fact that the profit is not realised, since the asset has only been revalued, not actually sold.

Reversal. The opposite of a *Conversion* and an example of an *Arbitrage* trade, where a future is sold and a synthetic future is purchased by buying a call *Option* and selling a put option with the same *Maturity* and *Strike price* on the same *Underlying asset*. Entered into when the *Put/call parity* relationship has broken down, and the future is relatively expensive to the synthetic.

Reverse cash and carry arbitrage. An *Arbitrage* trade entered into where a *Futures* contract is purchased and the underlying asset is sold in the cash market. Such a trade will be effected where the trader believes that the future is trading relatively cheaply to its *Fair value*.

Reverse repo. The position in a *Repurchase agreement* (repo) of a lender who has bought a *Bond* on the simultaneous agreement to sell it back again.

Review Panel. See *Financial Reporting Review Panel*.

Riba. In Islamic finance, *Riba* means interest, which is prohibited in Islamic law.

RIE. The acronym for a *Recognised Investment Exchange*.

Rights issue. An issue of shares for cash by a company to its existing shareholders on a basis that is *pro rata* to their existing shareholdings. The issue will normally be at a substantial discount to the current share price (typically between 20 per cent and 40 per cent discount). The rights issue is a means of implementing *Pre-emption rights*. In the case of a rights issue, existing shareholders will receive a *Provisional Allotment Letter (PAL)*, which tells them how many shares they have the right to subscribe for and the subscription price for the rights. Shareholders may exercise their rights and subscribe for the shares. Alternatively, they may sell the PAL to another person who can subscribe for the shares. This is known as selling the rights Nil paid. A third alternative is to take no action by the deadline for subscription. In this case, the company will sell the shares in the market, retain the subscription price and remit any excess proceeds from the sale to the shareholder who failed to take up his rights.

Ring. The term used to describe the area on the trading floor of the *London Metal Exchange (LME)* in which *Open outcry* trading takes place. Trading takes place throughout the day with each LME contract traded in specific five-minute periods known as 'rings'. Ring trading is so called because, in the LME, traders sit at fixed points around the circle. In other markets, the designated trading area is normally known as a *Pit*.

Ring member. A category of *LME* membership where the members are entitled to place traders in the *Ring* and thus trade metal contracts by *Open outcry*. As only ring members have this capacity, other categories of *LME* members must use the services of a ring member in order to effect trades in the ring.

Risk. In the context of investment, risk can be viewed as the possibility of loss or of returns that are less than expected. Risk is associated with uncertainty, and generally involves some quantification of possible outcomes. Overall investment risk is generally measured as the variation of actual and expected returns. However, a limitation of this approach which we should bear in mind is that it implies that higher upside variability of returns represents 'higher risk'. In reality, an investor will generally only view downside variability as unfavourable.

Risk reporting. The process of communicating the losses, exposure and risks to the appropriate level of management in the firm.

RNS. See *Regulatory News Service*.

ROCE. See *Return on Capital Employed*.

ROIE. The acronym for a *Recognised Overseas Investment Exchange*.

Rolling settlement. This is normal settlement for *CREST* eligible securities. The settlement date is based on a set number of business days (normally three business days) after the trade date, i.e. a trade dealt for T + 3 on a Monday would have an intended settlement date of Thursday.

RPI. See *Retail Prices Index*.

RPIX. The 'headline' *RPI* inflation figure takes into account *Mortgage* interest payments, on the basis that this is a typical cost for a household. There are, however, two alternative RPI measurements. RPIX excludes the impact of mortgage interest payments (known as the underlying rate of inflation) while *RPIY* excludes the impact of mortgage payments and indirect taxes, such as *Value added tax (VAT)*. See also *Consumer Price Index (CPI)*.

RPIY. RPIY is the *RPI* adjusted to exclude the impact of *Mortgage* payments and indirect taxes, such as VAT. See also *RPIX*.

Rule. Authorised firms must follow any *FSA Handbook* provision that has this status: rules generally place a binding duty on a firm and are indicated by the 'R' icon in the *Handbook*. A rule could be a quantitative specification, e.g. to do something within a specified number of days, but often rules are drafted in qualitative terms, e.g. 'to communicate in a way that clear, fair and not misleading'. The FSA's *Principles for Businesses* are rules. In general, *Private person* may sue under s150 *FSMA 2000* where they suffer loss resulting from a breach of a rule.

Running yield. See *Flat yield*.

RUR. See *Register Update Request*.

S

Standard and Poor's (S&P) produce a range of indices covering a wide range of US securities, the most widely known of which is the *S&P500 Index.*.

S&P 500 index. A share price index published by *Standard and Poor's* and covering 500 shares listed on the *New York Stock Exchange*. The index constituents are weighted according to their *Free float*. The shares represent some 80% of the total market capitalisation and, as such, are broadly representative of the US market. The index is seen globally as a broad indicator of the US *Equities* market.

Sadaqat. In Islamic finance, a voluntary charitable contribution, guided by the goodwill of the donor.

Safe custody investments. *Designated investments* that do not belong to a firm, but for which the firm is accountable. See also *Custody assets*.

Safe harbours. The defences against the civil offence of *Market abuse* set out in the *Code of Market Conduct*.

Safeguarded rights. Where *Protected rights* pension entitlements are transferred as a result of a pension sharing order in a divorce, they become 'safeguarded rights'. This means that they cannot be accessed before age 60 and no part can be taken in the form of cash at retirement.

Sale and repurchase agreement (repo). See *Repurchase agreement*.

Samurai bond. A yen bond issued in Japan by a foreign issuer.

Sarbanes-Oxley Act. US legislation passed in 2002 as a result of the corporate and accounting failings of firms such as Enron and Worldcom. The Act aims to protect US investors from further corporate collapses through a number of provisions including rules designed to improve the quality of financial reporting by public companies by increasing the responsibility of Chief Executive Officers (CEOs) and Chief Finance Officers (CFOs) for the accuracy of reports. The provisions of the Act apply to US and non-US companies that issue securities in the US, including UK companies with a dual listing in the US or which have shares traded via *American Depository Receipts (ADRs)*.

Sarbanes-Oxley Act: key provisions

- Accounting firms **prohibited** from providing most non-audit services for companies they audit.
- CEOs and CFOs to **certify** that accounts comply with reporting requirements.

- CEOs and CFOs to **certify** that there are no material mis-statements or omissions in financial reports.

Savings Certificates. A type of investment product issued by the UK Government's *National Savings and Investments (NS&I)* and backed by *HM Treasury*. These products are not specified investments under *FSMA 2000*.

Savings Directive. See *European Savings Directive*.

SBLI. See *Stock Borrowing and Lending Intermediary*.

Scale order. An order type which allows a gradual entry to or exit from the market. Such an order allows a trader to scale into or out of the market as he sees a trend confirmed in the market. For example, an order which stipulates 'buy five *FTSE 100 Index Futures* at 4200 with a further five contracts for each 20 point rise in the market' ensures that, as an upward trend occurs, the trader continues to build his position in accordance with his *Bullish* sentiment.

Scaling factor. Used in the calculation of the invoice amount for the settlement of *Futures*, the scaling factor converts the price quotation into the value of one contract. In most instances, the scaling factor will be the *Contract size*. For example, assume the *Exchange Delivery Settlement Price (EDSP)* for a lead futures contract is set by the exchange at $800. This is a price per tonne, and so to calculate the invoice amount for one contract, one would take the EDSP of $800 and multiply it by the scaling factor, which in this case is 25, the number of tonnes of lead in one futures contract. This gives an invoice amount of $20,000 which is the amount payable by the buyer to the seller.

Scanning loss. The initial margin calculated by *SPAN*. The scanning loss will be the worst case potential risk in a portfolio of *Derivatives* across a range of changes in price and volatility as calculated by the SPAN system.

Scarcity. The excess of human wants over what can actually be produced.

Schatz. Relatively short-term (usually two years) German Government debt.

Scrip dividend. An issue of shares to an investor *in lieu* of a cash dividend. Investors thereby increase the number of shares they hold in the company without incurring the costs of buying shares in the market. See also *Enhanced scrip dividend*.

Scrip issue. See *Bonus issue*.

SDRT. See *Stamp Duty Reserve Tax*.

SEAQ. The Stock Exchange Automated Quotation system of the *London Stock Exchange*. system used by *Market makers* to disseminate the prices at which they are prepared to trade in *Equities* and *Bonds* quoted on the exchange. The SEAQ system is the LSE's service for the fixed interest market and *AIM* securities that are not traded on either *SETS* or *SETSqx*. SEAQ a *Quote-driven competing Market maker* system. Member firms can take on the responsibilities of market-making, obliging them to quote their prices to other members (alternatively known as broker / dealers) who then decide whether or not to respond to them. These quotes are two-way prices, the lower of which is known as the *Bid price* and is the price at which the market-makers will buy stock; the higher price is the *Offer* (or ask *price*) and is the price which they will sell stock.

SEAQ crosses. A service which supplements the *Market-maker Quote driven system* by providing an alternative anonymous execution mechanism. It applies to all quote-driven FTSE 250 stocks. The execution price for the crosses is imported from the mid-price of market maker quotes at the time of each cross. There are three crosses each day with the final cross using the prices which form the official closing price. SEAQ crosses replaced the previous auction system, which was introduced in 2000. The system provides for anonymity, just like SETS, orders may be added or removed at any time of the trading day.

SEC. See *Securities and Exchange Commission*.

Secondary market. The market where investors trade securities among themselves, to be distinguished from the *Primary market*, where an issuer originally issues securities to investors.

Securities and Exchange Commission (SEC). The US Government agency with responsibility for regulating the securities industry. The SEC also has responsibility for regulating certain areas concerning *Derivatives*, namely stock options, stock index derivatives, currency transactions undertaken on exchanges and the *Chicago Board Options Exchange* (CBOE).

Securities lending. The process occurring when authorised institutions lend their assets and, when permitted, those of their clients, to market makers or other institutions through a network of intermediaries in exchange for a fee. Legal title to the securities passes from the lender to the borrower but the lender retains the benefits of ownership. This means that the lender continues to receive income and retains the right to sell the securities in the open market. The lender, however, loses the right to vote. Income will not be paid direct to the lender, as the name will have been removed from the company's register. Instead the income is claimed from and paid by the borrower. Securities lending and borrowing helps to provide *Liquidity* to the market and also facilitates the practice of *Short selling*.

Securitisation. A process of *Structured finance* by which financial instruments and assets are packaged together and made available as collateral for financial instruments which are backed by the cash flows of the *Underlying assets*. For example, residential *Mortgages* may be pooled together to create tradeable securities.

Security. (1) Broadly, an investment instrument, other than an insurance policy or an annuity, that is issued by an entity and constitutes debt or equity. For the purposes of most *FSA* rules, the specific definition of a security covers: shares, *Debentures*, government and public securities, *Warrants*, units in *Collective investment schemes*, *Stakeholder pension schemes*, *Personal pension schemes* and rights to or interests in investments. (2) The pledge of assets as collateral for a loan.

Security selection (or stock picking). Having decided on the *Asset allocation*, the investment manager must select specific securities within each asset category.

Segregation of duties. An *Internal control* which requires more than one person to complete a task. Lack of segregation can lead to problems being covered up accidentally or purposefully. Segregation should occur at both a macro level between front and back office and a micro level. Examples include a system in which one person banks cash, while another person maintains the cash book and a third performs reconciliations.

Selective marketing. See *Placing*.

Self-Invested Personal Pension (SIPP). A form of personal pension where the holder can select various types of investments including *Funds*, *Bonds*, direct shares and commercial *Property*, rather than being limited to the product range of a plan provider.

Self trading. See *Crossing*.

Serious Organised Crime Agency (SOCA). A government agency to whom the *Money Laundering Reporting Officer (MLRO)* will report suspected *Money laundering* activities. SOCA is a non-departmental agency sponsored by, but operationally independent from, the Home Office. SOCA is an intelligence-led agency with law enforcement powers and harm reduction responsibilities. 'Harm' in this context means the damage caused to people and communities by serious organised crime. SOCA was formed from the amalgamation of the National Crime Squad (NCS), National Criminal Intelligence Service (NCIS), that part of *HMRC* dealing with drug trafficking and associated criminal finance and a part of UK Immigration dealing with organised immigration crime (UKIS).

SETS. The Stock Exchange Electronic Trading Service of the *London Stock Exchange*. This is known as the order book, and allows trading of the most liquid shares in the UK. *Automatic matching* occurs on this electronic trading system. The strong recent growth in SETS trading is part of a long-term trend toward electronic trading on the Exchange's markets. In 2006, the Exchange rolled out electronic trading into mid-cap and *AIM* stocks using SETSmm. SETSmm had been launched in 2003 as the LSE's trading service for mid-cap FTSE 250 and liquid AIM securities. In October 2007, SETSmm and SETS were amalgamated to create a single platform for the trading of the constituents of the *FTSE All Share Index* and higher-traded AIM securities. The new service carries the name SETS and combines *Order-driven* trading with integrated *Market making*, guaranteeing two-way prices in all securities. It provides one approach (full execution including quotes) and one set of rules for trading of the more liquid UK securities. Order book trades in UK and Irish securities are covered by a *Central counterparty* operated by LCH.Clearnet (formerly known as the *London Clearing House*). Under the new 2007 arrangements, SETS offers market making in all stocks including those deemed to be 'liquid' under the *Markets in Financial Instruments Directive (MiFID)*. This provides customers with an on-exchange alternative to being a *Systematic Internaliser (SI)*. This enhancement provides users with a two-tier market structure for the trading of all *UKLA* listed securities – SETS for 'liquid' stocks and *SETSqx* for 'non-liquid' stocks as defined under MiFID.

SETSqx (SETS 'quotes and crosses'). A trading platform for securities less liquid than those traded on *SETS*. SETSqx replaced SEATS Plus in June 2007. Since 8 October 2007, all Main Market and EURM (EU Regulated Market) *AIM* equity securities not traded on a full order book are traded on SETSqx. They joined the Main Market and AIM securities with less than two *Market makers* which were added in June 2007 following the replacement of SEATS Plus. SETSqx combines a periodic electronic auction book with standalone *Quote-driven* market making. Electronic orders can be named or anonymous and, for the indicated securities, order book executions will be centrally cleared.

Settlement. The act of both buyer and seller (or their custodians) exchanging securities and cash in order to fulfil their contractual obligations. It is thus the process of transferring ownership of a security or other asset from the seller to the buyer in exchange for the equivalent value in cash. See also *Physical delivery* and *Cash settlement*.

Settlement due date. See *Intended settlement date*. The date on which payment is due for a trade.

Settlement queue. On *CREST*, each matched market transaction enters each member settlement queue at the start of the intended *Settlement* day, i.e. settlement queues are transactions awaiting settlement. There are two types of queue: cash queues (i.e. credit) and stock queues.

SGX. The Singapore Exchange which incorporates the *Derivatives* exchange of SIMEX.

Share capital. Part of *Shareholders' funds* in a company's *Balance sheet*. The share capital is given by the number of shares in issue (rather than the shares authorised for issuance) multiplied by the *Nominal value* per share.

Share premium account. A reserve that is part of *Shareholders' funds* in a company's *Balance sheet*. A share premium account arises when shares are issued at a premium to their *Nominal value*. For example, if shares with a nominal value of 100p are issued at a price of 150p, the share capital of the company will increase by the nominal value of 100p per share and the share premium account reserve will increase by 50p per share. The total of *Share capital* plus share premium account reserve therefore represents the total cash raised from shareholders by the company in the past.

Shareholders' funds. Also referred to as a company's net worth or equity, shareholders' funds is comprised of the issued *Share capital* of the firm together with retained reserves.

Sharia'a. The ethical framework of Islam, often referred to as Islamic law, and relevant to Islamic finance.

Short position. A term used to describe an open sold futures or options position, and to describe someone who sells a cash asset that is not owned by the person. Contrast with *Long position*.

Short hedge. A transaction that involves the sale of a futures contract, which is used to hedge a long cash market position. Such a transaction seeks to ensure that any decrease in the cash price on the subsequent cash market sale is offset by a profit on the futures position. Sometimes described as a producer's hedge.

Short run. In economics, a time period in which the amount of at least one input is fixed.

Short selling. The practice of selling securities one does not own. See *Securities lending.*

Short-term currency swap. A contract that commits two parties to exchange pre-agreed foreign currency amounts now and re-exchange them back at a given future date (the maturity date). The flows are capital only: no direct interest payment is involved.

Shortfall risk. The risk that an investment will fall short of a target figure.

Significant influence functions. *Controlled functions* that involve governing or managing the firm.

SIMEX. The Singapore International Monetary Exchange, now merged into the Singapore Exchange (SGX).

Single Settlement Engine (SSE). The SSE is central to *Euroclear's* business model to deliver a domestic market for Europe. Following the merger of CRESTCo and Euroclear in 2002, the SSE was the first result of the process of consolidating all Euroclear group systems and harmonising all Euroclear group services. In the longer term, the SSE will provide the basic infrastructure for transactions between all Euroclear group clients to be settled as internal book entries (as opposed to cross-system settlement), irrespective of which group *(International) Central Securities Depository ((I)CSD)* the counterparties use.

Single pricing. For *OEICs*, the obligation of an *Authorised Corporate Director* to provide one single price for both the purchase and the sale of the OEIC's shares.

Sinking fund. A pool of money set aside for the purpose of repaying a bond issue in instalments over its life. The bonds that are redeemed early (at *Par*) may be determined by drawing of lots. See also *Purchase fund* and *Bullet form*.

SIPP. See *Self-Invested Personal Pension*.

SIV. See *Structured Investment Vehicle*.

Socially responsible investment (SRI). An approach to investment which takes a proactive stance on social and environmental aspects of investment decisions. SRI *Funds* employ screens that eliminate stocks from a potential universe (negative screening), as well as seek to include a certain level of corporate social performance (positive screening), alongside corporate financial performance.

Soft commission. A type of inducement under which a guaranteed level of business is given in return for benefits such as research. There are rules with respect to the disclosure of such arrangements as well as to the type of benefits that may be supplied. The arrangements are now referred to as 'use of dealing commission' (*COBS* 11.6).

Soft commodities. In general, *Commodities* that can be grown or raised. Soft commodities are agricultural products including wool and cotton, and foodstuffs such as meats, cocoa, coffee, soya and sugar. Soft commodities have the characteristic of being renewable, usually on an annual cycle. Crops can be grown season after season. Many soft commodities are perishable and so must be consumed before deterioration makes them unuseable. This can make their prices highly volatile. Soft commodities prices are increasingly influenced by the growth in biofuels such as ethanol. See also *Hard commodities*.

Solvency. The ability to pay debts as they fall due.

Sovereign risk. See *Country risk*.

Sovereign wealth fund (SWF). An investment fund owned by a sovereign nation.

SPAN. Standard Portfolio Analysis of risk, a margining system used by the *LCH* to calculate initial margins due from and to its clearing members. SPAN is a computerised system that calculates the effect of a range of possible changes in price and *Volatility* on portfolios of *Derivatives*. The worst probable loss calculated by the system is then used as the *Initial margin* requirement. See also *Scanning loss*.

Special cum/ex. The purchase of securities currently trading ex-dividend/coupon on the market such that the next income stream is received by the buyer (special cum); or the purchase of securities trading cum dividend/coupon such that the next income stream remains the entitlement of the seller (special ex).

Special resolution. A shareholders' resolution at an *Annual General Meeting* or *Extraordinary General Meeting* which requires a 75% majority of votes cast in order to be approved. Special resolutions are usually matters of importance for the company and include, for example, resolution to wind-up the company. Where a special resolution is to be discussed, 21 calendar days' notice will usually need to be given of the meeting.

Specific risk. See *Unsystematic risk*.

Specific tax. A tax that is charged as a fixed sum per unit sold.

Specified investments. For regulatory purposes, those investments defined in the Regulated Activities Order (as amended). Only activities relating to specified investments are covered by *FSMA 2000*.

Speculator. An investor or trader hoping for large profits from risky positions, i.e. a risk taker. In contrast, a hedger is someone who wishes to reduce risk from an existing position. It is often the speculator who takes on the risk that has been transferred from the hedger.

Sponsor. An authorised person (usually a *LSE* member firm, a firm of accountants or a firm of solicitors) who is on the register of sponsors held by the *UK Listing Authority*. The role of the sponsor is to prepare companies for listing of their shares. The sponsor seeks to ensure that the company is suitable for listing and that directors are aware of their responsibilities as directors of a listed company. Where a company is planning to obtain a listing for debt securities, it needs a listing agent instead of a sponsor. The role of the listing agent is less onerous than that of a sponsor due to the nature of the securities involved.

Sponsored member. Certain investors such as private investors and institutions who are active traders, wanting to hold stock in *CREST* accounts but, lacking the direct technical access to CREST, can rely on another member or user of CREST. A sponsored member will appear in the register as the legal owner.

Spot. The price of an asset for immediate delivery.

Spot month margin. One of the adjustments made by the *SPAN* margining system to the *Initial margin* requirement. This increases the *Margin* requirement for products on certain exchanges as delivery for that product draws near. This occurs in order to ensure that customers contemplating taking the contract to delivery have allocated adequate funds to effect settlement, and also to force any less well-capitalised speculators out of the market, and thereby reduce short-term speculative pressures.

Spread. (1) The difference between the *Bid price* and *Offer price*, representing the expected profit of a *Market maker*. (2) The additional yield above a government benchmark yield required for the *Credit risk* of a *Corporate bond*. (3) The simultaneous purchase and sale of two very similar, but slightly different, *Derivatives* on the same *Underlying asset*. Generally, such trades are of limited risk due to the offsetting nature of the two contracts in the spread. *Intra-market spread* and *Inter-market spread* are spread trades involving *Futures* contracts. *Diagonal spread, Horizontal spread* and *Vertical spread* relate to *Option* spread trades.

Spread betting. The facility enabling bets to be placed on a range of outcomes, such as share prices, with either *Short* or *Long positions* being simulated by a bet. Financial spread betting is one form which is fairly popular in the UK, while many spread betting companies also accept bets on sports outcomes.

Spread margin. An adjustment made to the calculation of initial margin that takes account of offsetting risks in *Futures* contracts. Within the *SPAN* system, two types of spread margins are calculated: (1) An *Initial margin* that is levied to account for the possibility of an adverse move in the relationship between two delivery dates. This is necessary as, in the determination of the *Scanning loss*, this risk is ignored. (2) The inter-commodity spread credit takes account of the reduced risk of position, which consists of long and short futures in different, but related contracts, e.g. Brent crude/gas oil. The credit is deducted from the *Scanning loss*.

Spread order. An order in which a *Spread* transaction is described.

SRI. See *Socially Responsible Investment*.

Stabilisation. See *Price Stabilising Rules*.

Stag. An investor who applies for shares on a new issue, hoping to sell them at a profit immediately afterwards.

Stakeholder pension scheme. A type of pension plan which is similar to a *Personal pension scheme* except that charge caps apply. Establishing and operating a stakeholder pension scheme is a *Regulated activity* under *FSMA 2000*.

Stakeholder products. A suite of simple and 'risk-controlled' regulated products, including deposit accounts, *Collective investment schemes* and long-term insurance products with smoothed investment returns. Charge caps apply where appropriate, and firms are permitted to offer a basic level of advice on stakeholder products.

Stamp Duty. A tax levied on the purchaser of UK securities bought in paper form. The rate is 0.5% (1.5% on the creation of *Depository Receipts*) of the consideration value rounded up to the next £5. The liability arises on the settlement date.

Stamp Duty Reserve Tax (SDRT). A tax levied on the purchaser of UK securities bought in paperless form, i.e. via *CREST*. The UK rate is 0.5% (1.5% on the creation of *Depository Receipts*) of the consideration value rounded to the nearest penny. The liability arises on the trade date.

Standard deviation. A dispersion measure that is related to the *Arithmetic mean*. The idea behind the calculation is to establish how far each observed value falls from the mean, the standard deviation being a function of this divergence, and the *Variance* being the square of the standard deviation.

State Second Pension (S2P). An earnings-related pension scheme provided by the government to supplement the Basic State Pension. S2P replaced the former State Earnings Related Pension Scheme (SERPS) from April 2002.

Statements of Principle for Approved Persons. Seven principles that approved persons must adhere to when performing a controlled function – set out in the Box below. The first four principles apply to all approved persons. The final three only apply to approved persons who are performing a significant influence function.

Statements of Principle for Approved Persons

1 An approved person must act with integrity in carrying out his controlled function.

2 An approved person must act with due skill, care and diligence in carrying out his controlled function.

3 An approved person must observe proper standards of market conduct in carrying out his controlled function.

4 An approved person must deal with the FSA and with other regulators in an open and co-operative way and must disclose appropriately any information of which the FSA would reasonably expect notice.

5 An approved person performing a significant influence function must take reasonable steps to ensure that the business of the firm for which he is responsible in his controlled function is organised so that it can be controlled effectively.

6 An approved person performing a significant influence function must exercise due skill, care and diligence in managing the business of the firm for which he is responsible in his controlled function.

7 An approved person performing a significant influence function must take reasonable steps to ensure that the business of the firm for which he is responsible in his controlled function complies with the relevant requirements and standards of the regulatory system.

Statutory Money Purchase Illustration (SMPI). An annual projection of benefits that is required to be provided annually for members of a *Defined contribution pension scheme*, based on assumptions defined in legislation.

Sterling. The currency of the United Kingdom: pounds sterling.

Stock Borrowing and Lending Intermediary (SBLI). A Stock Exchange member firm which acts as brokers identifying pools of stock that are available for lending to other market participants by their beneficial owners.

Stock deposit. A transaction to deposit stock currently in paper form, i.e. held outside *CREST*, into dematerialised form within a *CREST member* account.

Stock Exchange Automated Quotation (SEAQ). See *SEAQ*.

Stock picking (or stock selection). See *Security selection*.

Stock Transfer Form. A legal document that is required to transfer ownership of registered securities settling in certificated form.

Stock withdrawal. A transaction to withdraw stock held within *CREST* in dematerialised form for holding outside CREST in paper form.

Stocks. See *Inventories*.

Stop limit order. An order type that essentially combines a *Stop order* and a *Limit order*. As with a stop order, a level is specified at which the order is activated. However, unlike a simple stop order, where once the order is activated it is merely traded at the prevailing market price, this order type also has a limit attached. The limit prevents the trader from paying more or receiving less than a particular specified price. For example, a buy stop on a *FTSE 100 index future* with a stop of 4000 and limit of 4010 means that if the market reaches 4000 the buy order is activated, but that the dealer should pay no more than 4010 for the future.

Stop order. An order that is activated when a stipulated market level is reached. Once the stop level has been reached by the market, the order becomes a *Market order* and trades at the prevailing market price, not necessarily the specified stop level. Stops to sell are entered below the market, stops to buy above the market. They are generally used to exit positions, unlike *MIT* orders, which are normally used to enter the market place.

STOXX 50. An index covering the top 50 shares quoted on European exchanges.

Strachan Review. A review of the *FSA's* enforcement processes, commissioned by the FSA's Board in 2005, following criticisms by the *Financial Services and Markets Tribunal* of the FSA's enforcement methods relating to cases of mis-selling of endowment policies. The review, which was led by David Strachan, advocated greater transparency of the enforcement process and separation of those staff from the Enforcement Division who investigate and prepare the case and those who make the decisions in contested cases, i.e. the *Regulatory Decision. Committee*. As a result, changes were made to the *FSA Handbook* in 2005.

Straddle. A type of *Option combination*, where a *Call option* and a *Put option* on the same *Underlying asset* with the same *Strike price* and *Expiry date* are either purchased (long straddle) or sold (short straddle). Straddles are generally entered into when a trader has a view on *Volatility* – either that it will increase (long straddle) or decrease (short straddle). Long straddles have limited risk and unlimited rewards, whereas short straddles have limited reward and unlimited risks.

Strangle. A type of *Option combination*, where a call option and a put option on the same *Underlying asset* with the same *Expiry date* but different *Strike prices* are either purchased (long strangle) or sold (short strangle). Strangles are generally entered into when a trader has a view on volatility, either that it will increase (long strangle) or decrease (short strangle). Long strangles have limited risk and unlimited rewards, whereas short strangles have limited reward and unlimited risks. When compared to *Straddles*, strangle premiums are generally lower and have their breakevens further apart, i.e. a greater market movement (*Volatility*) will be required to make a long strangle profitable or a short strangle unprofitable.

Stratified sampling. An approach to *Passive fund management* that involves choosing investments that are representative of the index. For example, if a sector makes up 16% of the index, then 16% of shares in that sector will be held, even though the proportions of individual companies in the index may not be matched. The expectation is that with stratified sampling, overall the 'tracking error' or departure from the index will be relatively low. The amount of trading of shares required should be lower than for full replication, since the fund will not need to track every change in capitalisation of a share. This should reduce transaction costs and therefore will help to avoid such costs eroding overall performance. Contrast with *Full replication*.

Strike price. See *Exercise price*.

Straight Through Processing (STP). The process of seamlessly passing financial information to all parties to the transaction process, from the investment manager's decision through to reconciliation, without manual handling or redundant processing. STP applies both within a firm and beyond, in respect of its external relationships with its clients, custodians and counterparties.

Strategic risk. The risk of loss due to a sub-optimal business strategy being employed. For instance, a new product strategy may be employed that fails to maximise the return on the investment made.

Strips (Separately Traded and Registered Interest and Principal Securities). The *Zero coupon bonds* that are traded result from the *Coupon stripping* of a bond.

Structured finance. A field of finance that is designed to transfer *Risk* and pool together small obligations using sometimes complex structuring methods. The performance of the resulting financial instruments depends on the cash flows created by the pooled obligations.

Structured Investment Vehicle (SIV). A *Fund* that seeks generate profits by borrowing through the issue of short-term *Commercial paper* while buying long-term securities at higher rates of interest. An SIV is 'evergreen' (open-ended), meaning that it hopes to stay in business indefinitely by buying new assets as existing assets mature. Given the rolling nature of its funding, an SIV is highly reliant upon maintaining its *Credit ratings*.

Sub-prime lending. Making of loans to borrowers who have a low credit status.

Subsidiarity. In relation to the *European Union*, the principle that matters should be decided at the lowest level possible. The EU should only act where Member States agree that action by individual countries is insufficient.

Subsidiary company. A company that is controlled by another company, referred to as its *Holding company*. *Control* is usually achieved either by owning shares with more than 50% of the voting rights in the subsidiary, or by having the right to appoint directors to the board who have a majority of voting rights on the board.

Substitutes. Two goods that are consumed as an alternative to each other, for example, tea and coffee. If the price of coffee rises, then the demand for tea will increase, as it now represents an alternative to coffee at a relatively lower cost.

Suitability report. A report which a firm must provide to a retail client if the firm makes a personal recommendation and the client: buys or sells shares/units in a regulated *collective investment scheme* or through an *Investment trust* savings scheme or investment trust *ISA* or *PEP*, buys, sells, surrenders, cancels rights in or suspends contributions to a *Personal pension plan* or *Stakeholder pension plan*; elects to make income withdrawals from a short-term annuity; or enters into a pension transfer or pension opt-out. A suitability report is required for all personal recommendations in relation to *Life policies*. The suitability report must, at least: specify the client's demands and needs; explain the firm's recommendation that the transaction is suitable, having regard to information provided by the client; and explain any possible disadvantages of the transaction to the client.

Suitability rules. Rules requiring that, when making a personal recommendation in relation to a *Designated investment* under *MiFID* obligations, firms must ensure that the advice/service is suitable, in the case of *Retail clients* and *Professional clients*. In order to provide suitable advice, firms must obtain sufficient information to give them a reasonable basis for believing that their recommendation meets the investment objectives of the client. When making personal recommendations or managing investments for professional clients, in the course of MiFID business, a firm is entitled to assume that the client has the necessary experience and knowledge, in relation to products and services for which the professional client is so classified. For non-MiFID business, suitability rules apply to business with retail clients.

Sukuk. In Islamic finance, the plural of Sakk, representing a partial ownership of assets. Sukuk are technically neither shares nor *Bonds* but have characteristics of both. Profit is based on the performance of the *Underlying assets* or projects.

Superequivalence. See *Gold plating*.

Supply. The quantity of a good that producers are prepared to supply to the market at a given price. Supply is an upward sloping function, determined by the costs of the company: as the price rises, producers will be prepared to supply more of that particular good.

Supply side economics. An approach to economic policymaking which advocates measures to improve the supply of goods and services, including the markets for labour and capital rather than measures to affect aggregate demand.

Swap. An agreement to pay or receive the difference between two cash flows such that the effect is to swap from one basis (e.g. fixed rated interest) to another (e.g. floating rate interest).

Switching. The act of a firm or adviser engaging in excessive trading in a *Packaged product* to generate commission. Switching contravenes the *Client's best interests rule*.

SWOT analysis. An exercise in strategic planning for an enterprise or venture which analyses the Strengths, Weaknesses, Opportunities and Threats involved.

Synthetic. A *Derivative* position that is created synthetically by using other derivative contracts. An example is the creation of a synthetic long *Future* by the purchase of a call *Option* and the sale of a put option with the same exercise price and expiry date. The ability to synthetically create any derivative position by the combination of other derivative positions leads to the concept of *Put/call parity*, which states that there is a relationship between option and futures prices.

Synthetic fund. A type of *Futures* and *Options* fund which is designed to perform in accordance with an index – often a stock index such as the *FTSE 100 Index*. It does not invest in the underlying securities themselves but instead uses *Derivatives* to gain the same exposure, for example by purchasing a FTSE 100 future instead of the underlying 100 shares. The fund is not geared and therefore losses are limited to the amount originally invested.

Systematic internaliser. An investment firm which deals on its own account by executing client orders outside a regulated market or *MTF*. *MiFID* requires such firms to publish firm quotes in liquid shares (for orders below *'Standard market size'*) and to maintain those quotes on a regular and continuous basis during normal business hours.

Systematic risk (or market risk). The risk presented by changes in general market conditions. All companies are affected by such conditions and therefore this is the type of risk that cannot be eliminated through *Diversification*. Contrast with *Unsystematic risk*.

T-bills. See *Treasury bills*.

T&C. The abbreviation for the *FSA's Training and Competence rules*. The purpose of the T&C Sourcebook is to support the *FSA's* supervisory function by supplementing the *Competent employees rule* for retail activities.

Table A. A model set of *Articles of Association* in the Companies Act 1985. If a company does not write its own articles, it is assumed that Table A rules will apply.

Takaful. Islamic insurance, comparable to mutual insurance.

Takeover Code. See *City Code on Takeovers and Mergers*.

Takeover Panel. The UK regulatory body responsible for policing of takeovers and mergers of public companies and certain private companies resident in the United Kingdom. The Panel issues and administers the *City Code on Takeovers and Mergers*. The Panel's central objective is to ensure fair treatment for shareholders in takeover bids. The Takeover Panel was given statutory authority in the Companies Act 2006 (CA 2006), with effect from January 2007. CA 2006 gives the Panel this authority in respect of all bids subject to the *Takeover code* and not only those to which the Takeover Directive applies. The Panel has statutory powers under CA 2006 to make rules on takeover regulation, to require disclosure of information and to impose sanctions on those who breach its rules. In practical terms however, these changes have made little difference to how the Panel operates.

Taker. The term used on the *LME* for an *Options* holder.

Tap stock. A tap issue is where the stock is issued on a *tranche* by *tranche* basis into the market, rather than all being issued at the same time. This may arise where the initial issue of the *Gilt* is not a success or when the issue is very large. Where the subsequent issues of the gilt are fairly large, they are referred to as *Tranches*. Smaller issues are referred to as tranchettes.

Taper relief. A relief reducing the rate of capital gains tax payable on gains made after April 1998. The rate of relief varies for business assets or personal assets. The general principle is that the longer the asset is held, the lower the rate of capital gains tax payable.

TAPO. Traded Average Price Option, an *Asian-style option* traded on the *LME*.

TARGET (Trans-European Automated Real-time Gross Settlement Express Transfer System). An interbank payment system for real-time processing of cross-border transfers throughout the *EU*. TARGET is not itself a funds transfer system, in that transfers cannot be fed directly into the system. TARGET's function is to link existing national systems. TARGET links sixteen national *Real Time Gross Settlement (RTGS)* systems and the payment mechanism of the European Central Bank.

Tax treaties. See *Double taxation agreements*.

TCF (Treating customers fairly). For the *FSA*, treating customers fairly (TCF) centres around firms operating a principle-based approach and delivering what they promised, having a sound ethical compliance culture, putting customers at the centre of their business thinking, and considering TCF in terms of pricing, people, products and processes.

Technical analysis (TA) (or chartism). The study of past and current price movements in order to be able to predict future price movements. TA focuses on identifying patterns and trends in the market, often using charts and other statistical techniques. Unlike *Fundamental analysis*, TA does not consider fundamentals such as macroeconomic factors. While the validity of TA is often questioned by those using fundamental analysis, TA is often used by traders for short-term trading decisions, as it does allow the trader to take account of the psychology of the markets, in other words, how other market participants are likely to act and react to market conditions.

Temporary document of title. A certificate acting as *prima facie* evidence of ownership of shares in the short term. Eventually the temporary document will be replaced by the permanent or definitive document of title. Examples of temporary documents of title include *Provisional allotment letters* and *Letters of acceptance*.

Tender. In relation to *Futures*, the act of giving notice to the Clearing House of the seller's intention to physically deliver in satisfaction of a futures contract.

Tender offer. A means of implementing an *Offer for subscription* or an *Offer for sale*. The issuing house invites applications for shares, where the applicant specifies both the number of shares that they wish to buy and the price that they are prepared to pay. After the applications have been made, the issuing house will identify the best price at which the shares can be sold. All applicants will pay the same *Strike price*, regardless of what price they tendered. However, applicants who tendered the highest prices will be awarded the shares in preference to those who tendered lower prices. For example, suppose that a company wished to issue 1,000 new shares and received three tenders: one for 600 shares at a price of 200p, one for 800 shares at 150p and one for 400 shares at 100p. The investor who tendered 200p would be issued with 600 shares and the investor who tendered at 150p would receive 400 shares. The strike price could be set at 150p and both investors would pay this price. The *strike price* could not exceed 150p, otherwise the investor who tendered 150p would not be prepared to buy the shares. In addition to being used in share markets, tenders are used along with *Auctions* for new issues of *Gilts*. See also *Fixed price offers* and *Bookbuilding*.

Term assurance. Insurance against an individual's life for a specific period or term (usually ten years or more). If death does not occur during the term, the policy lapses and there is no payout.

Term repo. A *Repo* in which the term (length) of the repo is predetermined as part of the agreement. After the time specified in the agreement, the funds lent to the borrower will be repaid with interest and the collateral will be returned to the borrower by the lender. This contrasts with an *Open repo*, where the repo remains open until either party to the contract decided to terminate it.

Terminal value (or future value). The value of an investment at the end of a period of time, having accumulated and re-invested returns over that period.

Threshold conditions. Conditions relating to legal status, location of offices, any close links with another entity, adequate resource, and suitability, which an applicant for authorisation by the *FSA* must meet. The threshold conditions are set out in the Threshold Conditions Sourcebook (COND) in the *FSA Handbook* and also in Schedule 6 of *FSMA 2000*.

Tied agent (under *MiFID*). See *Appointed representative*.

Thin market. A market with little trading and poor liquidity.

Tick. The minimum permitted price movement in a futures or options contract. For example, if the tick for a wheat contract were 5p, this would mean that the price of the contract could move in multiples of 5p only. See also *Tick value*.

Tick value. The monetary value that a one tick movement on one futures contract represents, i.e. the profit or loss that such a price movement causes. Tick value is the product of multiplying the tick by the contract size. For example, if the tick for a wheat contract were 5p and a contract is for 100 tonnes, the tick value of a wheat contract is £5 (100 × 5p).

Ticker page. A page of a dealing screen that gives details of recent trades that have been completed on a chronological basis.

Tied agent. See *Appointed representative*.

Time and sales report. A record kept by the exchange of the quotations and trades dealt in the market by time.

Time decay. The propensity of *Time value* for an *Option* to erode as expiry draws near. Time decay is not linear: in the early life of an option time decay occurs slowly, but the rate of time decay increases as *Expiry* becomes closer. Time decay acts to the benefit of *Writers* of options and to the detriment of holders of options.

Time spread. See Horizontal spread.

Time value. In relation to *Options* and *Warrants*, the amount by which the total value, price or *Premium* of the option or warrant exceeds its *Intrinsic value*. For example, suppose that Call option has an exercise price of 100p and an option premium of 80p when the share price is 150p. The intrinsic value of the option is 50p (150p − 100p). The time value is the amount by which the premium exceeds 50p, i.e. 30p. If an option has no intrinsic value, its premium is entirely time value.

Timely execution. Transaction of a customer order as soon as is reasonably practicable the circumstances.

Tipping off. The offence of providing information to another person that is likely to prejudice an investigation into drug trafficking, terrorist activity or serious criminal conduct.

Tip sheets. Publications solely containing investment advice. Unlike newspaper publication (media tip sheets), publication of tip sheets by firms requires authorisation.

Total cost. For a given level of output, total cost comprises total fixed cost *plus* total variable cost.

Total Expense Ratio (TER). A standardised measure of a fund's charges.

Touch price. The best prices being offered in the market for a particular share. For example, if there are two *Market makers* registered in a stock, one of which is quoting 510-515 and the other 512-517, this indicates that the first market maker is prepared to buy at a price of 510p and sell at a price of 515p. The second market maker is prepared to buy at 512p and sell at 517p. The best price at which a customer can sell shares is 512p and the best price at which he can buy shares is 515p, giving a touch price of 512-515. This will be displayed on the touch strip on the *SEAQ* screen.

Tracker fund (or index tracker fund). A fund that passively tracks an index: see *Passive fund management*.

Trade bills. A form of IOU issued by a company used primarily for commercial rather than investment purposes. Examples include bills of exchange and letters of credit. Trade bills are not specified investments under *FSMA 2000*.

Trade Registration System (TRS). A real-time trade matching and administration system, which facilitates post-trade processing and position maintenance and is used by *LIFFE* and *ICE Futures* markets. Details of each trade are fed into the system through LIFFE CONNECT™ and are then assigned to accounts or allocated to other members.

Trade report. A report of a trade carried out on an exchange made to the exchange usually within three minutes of the trade by the senior party or seller. Details of the trade will be published subject to certain criteria so as to provide market transparency. This will enable the rest of the market to see what is happening to prices. This is separate from requirements for *Transaction reporting*.

Trade reporting period. The period during each working day (07:15-17:15) when the *LSE* will accept trade reports.

Traded options. *Options* with standardised features that are traded on an exchange. Contrast with over-the-counter (OTC) options, which are tailor-made for each investor's requirements.

TradElect™. The overall name for the London Stock Exchange's new trading system, designed to deliver enhanced levels of performance, reliability and scalability. The revamped platform will increase capacity fivefold, allowing the LSE to handle 3,000 messages per second as against 600 previously. The time taken to process an order will be cut to about 10 milliseconds, from 140 milliseconds previously. The LSE hopes that the new system will bring in more orders from *Hedge funds* and investment banks running algorithmic trading systems. As well as being able to handle higher volumes, TradElect™ is able to offer lower fees, and thus compete with new entrants such as the *Project Turquoise* group of investment banks. The introduction of TradElect™ in June 2007 marked the final and most significant phase of the LSE's four-year system upgrade project known as Technology Roadmap (TRM).

Tranche. Issue of more of an existing gilt or part of an issue of any security.

Transaction reporting. A report of a trade carried out on an exchange made to the exchange, usually by the end of that day. This is for regulatory purposes, enabling an *RIE* to monitor for *Market abuse*.

Transfer Club. A scheme to which many public sector pension schemes belong, providing improved terms on transfer between member schemes.

Transfer Value Analysis System (TVAS). A system required by the *FSA* to be used to produce a detailed report on a proposed transfer from an *Occupational pension scheme* to either a Section 32 arrangement or a *Personal pension scheme*. See also *Critical yield*.

TRAX. The trade reporting system used in the *Eurobond* markets.

Treasury bills (also known as T-bills). When issued by the UK Government, they usually have a maturity of 91 days. Treasury bills pay no interest and hence are issued at a discount to nominal value. The minimum nominal value of UK T-bills is £25,000. UK Treasury bills are usually denominated in sterling but may also be denominated in euro. Treasury bills are also issued by governments in other countries, such as the US Government.

Treasury bonds (or T-bonds). Long-term bonds issued by the US Government, with a life of more than ten years.

Treasury notes (or T-notes). Medium-term notes issued by the US Government, with a life between two and ten years.

Treating Customers Fairly. See *TCF*.

Treaty rights. European Single Market Directives do not cover the full range of authorisable activities. Therefore, in the absence of passporting rights, *FSMA 2000* provides for Treaty rights as a mechanism for EEA/UK firms to conduct regulated activities in UK/EEA states without the need for separate licensing. Treaty rights are less fully defined than passporting rights and have been the subject of developing EU case law in the EU. In practice, as the scope of the passporting Directives has expanded, these Treaty rights are being used less and less.

Trigger page. A dealing screen page showing details of the price movements on the day for *FTSE 100 stocks*. If a price change is in blue, this indicates a rise in price over the day. If it is in red, this indicates a fall. Green indicates no change.

Trivial commutation. The permitted commutation to a lump sum of relatively small pension arrangements held by an individual, subject to specified limits.

TRS. See *Trade Registration System*.

Trustee. A person who is the legal owner of assets but is holding them on behalf of another person who is to receive the benefit from the assets, i.e. the beneficiary. The legal owner is holding the assets on trust for the beneficiary and is referred to as a trustee. Trustees have legal obligation to manage and invest the assets appropriately on behalf of the beneficiary.

Trustee Act 2000. An Act of Parliament setting out the rules about trust investment policy and imposing conditions on trustees with regard to a duty of care to manage. The main elements include the following. A duty of care: the Act creates a general duty for trustees to exercise reasonable care in investments. Investment powers: trustees may make any investment of the kind that they could if the funds were their own, with the exception of overseas land. Investment duties: trustees must review their investments on a regular basis, and obtain proper advice, and exercise due consideration as to whether there is a need for diversification of the funds.

Turquoise. See *Project Turquoise*.

Uberrimae fidei. 'Of the utmost good faith': a principle applying to insurance contracts, that the proposer has an obligation to disclose material matters in full.

UCITS. See *Undertakings for Collective Investment in Transferable Securities*.

UITF. See *Urgent Issues Task Force*.

UK Listing Authority (UKLA). See *Competent authority*.

Ultra vires. See *Legal risk*.

Uncrossing algorithm. A mathematical process for determining a single price at which limit and market orders entered in a SETS auction call period will be matched. No input or deletion is permitted during the running of the uncrossing algorithm.

Undated gilts. Government bonds that do not have a predetermined maturity date (e.g. the UK Government's 3½% War Loan). Such *Gilts* are sometimes referred to as irredeemables since it is unlikely that the government will choose to redeem them due to the low interest rates the existing issues are paying.

Underlying asset. The security, stock, commodity, index or future upon which an options or futures contract is based.

Undertakings for Collective Investments in Transferable Securities (UCITS). Funds (*Unit trusts* or *OEICs*) that can be marketed throughout the *European Economic Area (EEA)* provided they are registered with their domestic regulator as such.

Underwriter. A market participant who agrees to buy a new issue at a specified price if no one else is prepared to purchase the securities offered. The underwriter will receive commission to compensate him for the risk taken that he will have to buy an unsuccessful issue and could lose money as a result.

Unemployment. The percentage of the total labour force that is out of work. There are various categories of unemployment within economics. In classical theory, unemployment is simply a supply and demand phenomenon within the labour markets. An excess of labour supply over demand represents the unemployed. By this theory, workers are unemployed because their wage requirements are too high. Frictional unemployment is where individuals transfer between jobs and are temporarily unemployed. Structural unemployment occurs where there is a fundamental shift in the nature of the demand for labour – as, for example, the decline of shipbuilding in the North East of England. As the industry declines, skilled workers become unemployed.

Unit trust. A form of *Collective investment scheme*. A form of trust in which the *Trustees* of the trust are holding the assets on behalf of the unit holders. The assets are invested by the unit trust manager on behalf of the trustee. Investors buy units in the unit trust, which then uses the money raised to invest in a range of specified investment areas. If investors wish to redeem their units, they do so by selling them back to the manager of the unit trust. As a result, the unit trust will have to sell some investments to generate the cash required to repurchase the units. This gives rise to the description of unit trusts as *Open-Ended*; the size of the unit trust may vary and is determined by the level of new units purchased relative to units redeemed. See also *Investment trusts*, *Undertakings for Collective Investments in Transferable Securities* and *Open-Ended Investment Companies*.

Unmatched transaction. A transaction for which details reported by the relevant counterparties cannot be agreed because the details are inconsistent. An unmatched transaction also results from only one party having input details. Settlement cannot then occur.

Unregulated collective investment scheme. A collective investment scheme that is unrecognised under FSMA 2000 and therefore cannot be freely marketed to the general public.

Unsystematic risk. Risk arising from the unique circumstances of a specific security. Unsystematic risk can be eliminated through diversification. It may alternatively be characterised as risk arising as a result of the trade between companies. By investing in both companies, we can eliminate this variability from our portfolio. Also referred to as *Idiosyncratic risk* or *Specific risk*. Contrast with *Systematic risk*.

Unweighted index. An index where all the constituents of the index are equally weighted when calculating the index value. This method has a weakness in that it tends to overstate the importance of the smaller constituents of the index. Examples of unweighted indices include the much-followed *Dow Jones Industrial Average*, the *Nikkei 225* and the now little used FTSE Ordinary indices. See also *Weighted index*.

Upstairs trading. See *Block trade*.

Urgent Issues Task Force. A sub-committee of the Accounting Standards Board that is set up to deal with urgent accounting issues on an *ad hoc* basis. It produces *Abstracts*, which are essentially mini *Accounting Standards* and must be followed by companies when preparing their accounts.

Variance. The square of the *Standard deviation* of a set of values.

Variation margin. The profits or losses on open positions that are calculated daily in the process of *Marking to market* and then paid or collected. For example, variation margin is calculated at the end of each business day by *LCH.Clearnet*, and then collected the next business day via the PPS system. Unlike *initial margin*, which is kept by the clearing house until a position is closed out or reaches expiry, variation margin is merely collected from the loss-making side of the contract by the clearing house, and then paid to the profit-making side of the contract.

Venture capital. A type of *Private equity* investment, where the investment is generally in the equity shares of an unquoted company. Venture capital providers are typically investment banks or professional investors that specialise in raising funds for new business ventures. These organisations are therefore typically providing capital for fairly risky ventures, in the hope of achieving above average returns. The 'venture capitalist' investors often assume a role in management of the investee company.

Vertical spread. An option spread, where one option is purchased and another option is sold, both options being on the same underlying asset and having the same expiry but different *Strike prices*. The spread will be constructed with either calls or puts. Where the lower strike option is purchased and the higher strike option is sold, the spread is known as a bull spread. Where the lower strike option is sold and the higher strike option is purchased, the spread is called a *Bear spread*.

Viatical settlement. The sale of a life policy to a 'viatical company' for cash by a terminally person. Viatical companies' activities are regulated under FSMA 2000.

virt-x. A *Recognised investment exchange* in the UK, competing with the *LSE* as a centre for share dealing. virt-x is an order-driven system for European *Blue chip* securities. It offers single system that trades in the constituents of all the European blue chip indices bringing the total number of stocks traded on virt-x to over 600, representing approximately 80% European market capitalisation. Based in London, virt-x was created in 2001 through collaboration between Tradepoint Financial Networks plc (now renamed virt-x plc), the Consortium (TP Group LDC) and SWX Swiss Exchange to provide an efficient and cost-effective pan-European blue chip market. The virt-x market is based on an integrated trading, clearing and settlement model intended to simplify the trading process and to significantly reduce the costs associated with cross-border trading.

Volatility. (1) Variability, usually with reference to returns available on a security (2) The risk that the price of a bond will vary due to change in interest rates. See also *Implied Volatility* and *Historic Volatility*.

War Loan. An undated UK government bond (*Gilt*) issued by the UK Government, for which the full name is 3.5% War Loan.

Warrant. An instrument that gives its holder the right to subscribe for new shares in a company at an agreed price (the *Strike price* or *Exercise price*) on an agreed date or range of dates. Warrants may be issued by the company itself or, in the case of *Covered warrants*, by a financial institution.

Weekly Official Intelligence. A *London Stock Exchange* publication issued each Saturday which contains official notices and detailed information on meetings, dividends, directors' dealings and other events for all quoted securities.

Weighted index. An index where the impact of each of the index constituents is weighted, usually by reference to the value of each constituent (e.g. *Market capitalisation*). To give a simple illustration, a share price index covering two companies, where the first company has a total market capitalisation of £3,000,000 and a share price of £3.00 and the second company has a market capitalisation of £6,000,000 and a share price of £6.00 would have a weighted value of £5.00 (3/9 × 3.00 + 6/9 × 6.00). By contrast, an *Unweighted index* would have a value based on the simple average of £4.50. Most indices, including the *FTSE 100 Index* and the *S&P 500 Index*, are market capitalisation weighted.

When issued basis. See *Grey market*.

Whistleblowing. The process whereby an employee seeks to make a protected disclosure to a regulator, in good faith, of information which shows that their employer is committing or deliberately concealing an activity covered by the *Public Interest Disclosure Act 1998*.

Whole of life policy. A *Life assurance* policy where a capital sum will be paid upon the death of the policyholder, whenever that may be.

Winding-up order. A Court instruction for a company to cease trading. The *FSA* has powers to present a petition for a winding-up order in relation to a firm either on grounds of insolvency or if it would be just and equitable for the firm to be wound-up.

Withholding tax. Tax that is deducted from payments to non-residents, usually in the form of a standard rate of tax applied to dividends or other payments by companies. The tax withheld may be reclaimable under bilateral *Double taxation agreements* between countries.

With profits. A form of assurance-based contract offering returns that are 'smoothed' to reflect long-term investment performance.

Working capital. For an enterprise, the excess of current assets, which may include *Inventories* (stocks), receivables (debtors) and cash, over current liabilities – in other words, *Net Current Assets*.

World Bank. A source of financial and technical assistance to developing countries, made up of the International Bank for Reconstruction and Development (IBRD) and, focusing on the poorest countries, the International Development Association (IDA). The World Bank supplements private finance and lends money on a commercial basis for capital projects, usually direct to governments or government agencies.

World Trade Organisation (WTO). A global international organisation dealing with the rules of trade between nations. The WTO agreements were negotiated and signed by the bulk of the world's trading nations and ratified in their parliaments. The WTO's overall goal is to assist free trade, helping producers of goods and services, exporters and importers conduct their business.

Wrap account. A product allowing a range of products, such as ISAs, SIPPs and holdings of funds, to be held in a single account, which can usually be accessed online. Typically, a single annual management fee will be charged. The individual can view the value of his or her assets and asset allocation based on up-to-the-minute data.

Writer. A person who executes the opening sale of an *Option*. The writer sells the option to the holder, giving the holder the right to exercise. The writer receives the premium from the holder as compensation for the level of risk he is willing to take on board.

Yankee bond. A US dollar bond issued in the US by a foreign issuer.

Yellow Book. This used to be the informal name for the *Listing Rules*, so called because of the original colour of its cover.

Yield to maturity. See *Gross redemption yield*.

Z

Zakat. In Islamic finance, an obligatory donation to charity for those who can afford it – 2.5% of wealth when based on a lunar calendar year, 2.5775% for a solar calendar year.

Zero coupon bond. A bond issued at a discount to its face value, normally par. The level c discount given will be based upon the period between purchase and the bond's redemptior date. No interest is paid on the bond. See also *Deep discount bond*.